SELF-COACH YOUR WAY TO AN AMAZING LIFE

Self-Coach Your Way to an Amazing Life

After Incarceration

LISA LANDRIGAN

Cornerstone Consulting Services

Copyright © 2021 by Cornerstone Consulting Services, LLC

All rights reserved. No part of this book may be reproduced in any manner whatsoever without written permission except in the case of brief quotations embodied in critical articles and reviews.

First Printing, 2021

Table of Contents

Introduction

Part 1 Principles of Self Coaching

    Chapter 1   Awareness & Self-Awareness
    Chapter 2   The T.R.U.T.H. Tool
    Chapter 3   Managing Your Thoughts
    Chapter 4   Tools for Self Coaching

Part 2 Life After Incarceration

    Chapter 5   Basic Needs
    Chapter 6   Reentry Toolbox
    Chapter 7   Employment
    Chapter 8   Support Systems
    Chapter 9   Physical & Mental Health
    Chapter 10   Communication and Problem Solving

Conclusion

Introduction

If you are reading this book, I'm going to assume you are in a place you would rather not be. If your circumstances have resulted in loss of freedom for any amount of time, this book is for you. I'm writing this book for you and to you. My experience with the prison environment comes from both my professional life and my personal life. Professionally, I am a retired corrections worker with over twenty years of experience. I worked in both the state and federal prison systems. Personally, I have loved ones who struggle with addiction and who have been in and out of prison several times.

This book is about what I learned from working inside a prison and what I've come to realize by watching my loved ones caught in the revolving door of incarceration. I was not searching for a career inside a prison; it found me. I imagine that is how a lot of staff find themselves working inside a prison. Nonetheless, it proved a good career for me. It allowed me to grow and become a better person. Working inside a prison and learning to see the good in every single person brought me to where I am today. Working in a prison helped me find my voice, my passion, and my purpose.

About halfway into my career, my professional life and my personal life became intertwined. My oldest son got in trouble when he was 19 and went to jail. He was sentenced to 120 days shock incarceration. He continued in and out of prison for ten years. During this time, my youngest son began acting out and experimenting with illegal substances. We tried every type of intervention program we had access to before he turned 18 in hopes of preventing him from going to prison. None of them worked. He went to prison and remains there today. His lifestyle, which was fueled by his addiction, landed him in state prison to serve a fifteen-year sentence.

Many people may assume that most of the individuals in prison came from chaotic, abusive, or violent homes, which then led them to make bad decisions. My son's going to prison proved this theory wrong for me. I was already working at a prison when my sons started committing crimes. I was and still am a law-abiding citizen. Those who know me will say that I am a rule follower to the extreme. I never liked getting in trouble when I was a kid, and that carried into my adult life. How did I raise kids who were seemingly the opposite of me in that respect? That is the question that haunted me for many years. My thoughts of failing as a parent resulted in so much guilt and shame that I couldn't even talk about my kids to my friends, and I sure didn't want anyone to know they were in jail. I eventually realized that I was carrying guilt for someone else's decisions. I have no control over what others decide, not even my own kids. Over time and by realizing this, I no longer feel like I failed as a parent, and I am able to understand that all of us are on individual journeys, even those we love the most.

What I have learned, and the main focus of this book, is a concept I'm calling the T.R.U.T.H. tool. It's a basic strategy for recognizing how we're thinking. It shows us how results in our life are directly linked to our thoughts and feelings — or, in reverse, our thoughts and feelings ultimately produce our results. I discovered this process several years ago and it has changed my life. Using the T.R.U.T.H. tool with everyday situations, as well as in challenging situations, helps me stay focused on the best possible outcomes that are within my power to achieve.

Working inside a prison and having a child in prison gave me ample opportunities to use the T.R.U.T.H. tool. Both of my sons are kind, caring, compassionate, and genuinely good people. As staff in a prison, I was never one of the tough guys or someone who believed in "locking them up and throwing away the key." Even before my sons got in trouble, I firmly believed in second chances. I already believed people could change. I already viewed incarcerated people as people who had made bad decisions, and I certainly didn't believe they deserved to be punished for the rest of their lives, or at least the majority didn't. I have made plenty of bad decisions in my lifetime, and I would hate to be punished for the rest of my life for those decisions. If I would not want this for myself, it only makes sense that I would not want that for anyone else.

What I realize now is that staff in a prison are supervising a population of people who have been deemed dangerous and bad, when in fact only a small percentage of incarcerated people are violent offenders. It is sometimes difficult to separate out the ones who might cause harm to others from those who won't, so it may seem easier and safer for everyone to treat all inmates like they are dangerous and capable of violence. This environment certainly does not promote self-improvement or self-worth.

This book is divided into two sections. Part 1 focuses on self-coaching tools and practices that will help you stay focused on what you need and desire to live your best life. Part 2 focuses on life after incarceration and provides examples of many useful forms and letters. My hope in this book is to give you tools and information you will need to better prepare for your release. Wouldn't it be nice if you didn't have to ask someone to help you get information that you feel is important to your success after prison? If you apply the concepts and use the information in this book, I am certain you will gain a sense of independence and accomplishment because YOU are doing the work. This book is an attempt to help you understand that your current situation or past mistakes do not define you. You aren't less than or unworthy because of your past decisions. Everyone has made mistakes. Someone once said the only difference between someone in prison and someone out of prison is that the person in prison got caught. I believe there is a lot of truth to this statement.

Part One

Part 1: Principles of Self-Coaching

One thing we all have in common is that we have experienced a life change that has caused pain or discontent. Whether it be a divorce, death of a loved one, or loss of a job, life changes happen, and some are beyond our control. Negative feelings associated with a life change are signals that something different is being desired. Each of us, depending on what is causing our pain or unhappiness, may choose to hire a formal coach or counselor to help us process our feelings. Another option that we don't really think about, but is always with us, is the ability to self-coach ourselves through these times.

Self-coaching is based on the simple fact that no one knows you better than yourself. You know what you like, what you don't like, what makes you happy, and what makes you sad. Knowing this, doesn't it make sense that you should be the person in control of your life? *Are* you in control of your life?

In this section, you will be introduced to the principles of self-coaching. Understanding and mastery of these principles will enable you to start creating your amazing life. I encourage you to take the time to fill out the worksheets that are provided at the end of some of the chapters. Take notes and write down your thoughts as you read the material so you can reflect later. As you read and study this material, ask yourself, "What do I really want?"

Chapter 1

Awareness and Self-Awareness

What does awareness mean to you? Does it simply mean that you're awake and functioning? Many people live day in and day out believing they are aware of what's going on around them when the exact opposite is true. It's easy to get so caught up in "the next thing" that we aren't truly aware of the present moment. It is just as easy to stay focused on the past, which also keeps us from being fully aware of the present moment.

Webster's dictionary defines "awareness" as the quality or state of being aware: knowledge and understanding that something is happening or exists. Being aware of what is happening around us seems like a simple thing to do. You can see things around you, but that doesn't mean you are aware of each thing. I can look at a tree and be thinking about what I'm going to do this weekend. I can see the tree, but I'm not aware of or thinking about the tree.

Imagine this: You're sitting outside daydreaming about somewhere you would rather be. Your thoughts take you away to another place. You are so deep in thought that you don't hear the birds, see the trees or flowers, or hear your buddy next to you ask you a question. In this scenario you are not aware of your present surroundings.

Can you think of situations or conversations you've had recently where you weren't fully paying attention? Paying attention, being aware, being in the present moment — these phrases all have the same meaning. Have you ever been on the phone with a bunch of people around you being loud? I imagine most of us have. How hard is it to stay focused on what the person on the phone is saying? It's easy to understand why it might be difficult to stay aware during this phone conversation. Now, imagine being on the phone having that same conversation with complete quiet around you. How hard is it to be aware of the conversation now? It's easy, right? It's easy unless your thoughts are distracting you.

Thoughts are sneaky. They creep in and capture our attention. Most of the time we don't even know it's happening until we "wake up" and realize we didn't hear what the person talking to us just said. Has this ever happened to you? It's happened to me more than I care to admit. The more you practice being aware, the more quickly you will catch and dismiss your thoughts when they are trying to shift your attention away from the present moment.

Being in the present moment does not mean you should not set goals and work towards them. Setting goals is crucial so we can continue to grow and learn and achieve our dreams. In a book called *The Slight Edge*, author Jeff Olsen explains it by saying "Our growth potential is never stationary. Every moment of every day, our personal growth is either moving forward or backward."

Being self-aware is an awareness of one's own personality or individuality. To be self-aware is to know certain things about yourself. The first level of self-awareness is simple: You know what you want and need to be you. In other words, you know what makes you feel all the emotions; happy, sad, mad, excited, etc. I would like to invite you to take self-awareness to the next level. Go a little deeper and ask why those "things" that govern your emotions create the feelings of happiness, sadness, anger, or excitement.

Think about something that would make you feel happy. It could be something as simple as getting to spend time with your best friend. Why does this make you happy? Your answer might be because you and your friend have a lot in common and like to talk about all these things. It might be because your friend pushes and challenges you to be stronger, smarter, etc. Your thoughts about why spending time with your best friend makes you happy are what cause the emotion of happiness to take place. This concept will be explained in more detail in the next chapter.

Becoming self-aware gives you complete control over your life. Once you understand that what you think determines every single outcome you experience and that you have the power to change your thoughts, you can live from a place of intention and purpose. Yes, this is absolutely true, and it is possible for each and every one of us. We are in the driver's seat of our own life. If you don't like the way things are going for you, change your thoughts and you will definitely change your life. For most of us, this is not easy. We have years and years of old beliefs and habits, and we think these have made us who we are. Even if we don't like who we are, letting go of these beliefs can seem impossible. I've learned if you take it one moment and one thought at a time, these old beliefs and habits will slowly start to fade and will be replaced with new ones that promote a happier and healthier life.

When you start to do this, you are well on your way to becoming more self-aware. You will discover what truly motivates and inspires you. You will wake each morning and be excited to begin your day. You will look for opportunities to learn and grow. You will move towards and begin to live from a place that is authentic to you. Your confidence will increase. You will begin to make decisions that will move you in the direction of your dreams and desires. If you are questioning whether or not this is true or just a bunch of "feel good" mumbo jumbo, then I challenge you to give it a try. Try it, and if it works then you will be on your way to your best life. What have you got to lose?

If you want to read more on being aware, Eckhart Tolle is an amazing author who explains why we must be present in the "now" moment to experience our best life. In the beginning, you might find it difficult to be fully aware all the time. Don't worry, because even those who have practiced this for a very long time have not mastered being aware every minute of every day. The important thing to remember is that this will get easier the more you practice it. You will soon start recognizing more quickly when you are not aware, and you can switch your focus to the present moment.

Chapter Notes & Key Takeaways:

Chapter 2

The T.R.U.T.H. Tool

Now we will go deeper into how every single result we get in our life is a result of our thoughts about circumstances we encounter. You will be introduced to my T.R.U.T.H. tool, and I will explain how using this tool when making decisions is life changing. Other authors and teachers have also used this concept to show how our thoughts, feelings, and actions lead to the majority of results we've had in our life. If you get only one takeaway from this book, my hope is for it to be how to apply this T.R.U.T.H. tool to every single decision you make.

The T in the T.R.U.T.H. tool stands for "The Thing." We all encounter "things" each and every day. When we wake up each morning and start our day, things begin to happen. It might be that we lie in bed for another hour and are late for work, or we can get out of bed and get ready and be on time. These "things" can be easy, or they can be difficult. Whether or not to be late for work is an easy situation for some. The person who loves their job and had a good night's sleep probably won't give much thought as to whether or not they will get up and be on time for work. But what about the person that was up most of the night and also does not like their job? Can you see how the same situation is more difficult for them? The T or "Thing" represents everything that occurs in our lives. In this case being at work on time is the "Thing." These things are always neutral, and we can't control them. The "Thing" is not good or bad until we move to the next step in the T.R.U.T.H. tool. It doesn't matter how simple or how complex the "Thing" is, you can use the T.R.U.T.H. tool to make it work best for you.

The R in the T.R.U.T.H. tool stands for "Realizing Thoughts." In the last chapter I introduced the concept that our thoughts are the driving force behind everything we experience. Sticking with the "Thing" of being on time for work, let's look at the thoughts each of these people might have. The person who got a good night's sleep and loves their job wakes up and thinks, "Ah, it's another day, and I get to make money doing what I love to do." Another thought they might have is, "Wow, I slept really great last night, and I feel amazing." The other person, who didn't sleep well and who doesn't like their job, wakes up to their alarm and their first thought is, "Are you serious — it's already time to get up? I hardly slept at all, and I'm so tired." As they lie in bed, their next thought is, "I can't deal with my job when I'm this tired." Can you see how the same situation — that it's time to get up and get ready for work — has produced two completely different thought processes? Realizing Thoughts is key to understanding that your thoughts about the Thing are what make it a positive or a negative situation. Remember, the Thing is completely neutral until we put a thought with it.

The U in the T.R.U.T.H. tool is "Understand Feelings." You know what the Thing is, and you are Realizing Thoughts. Now it's time to Understand Feelings. Using the same situation, let's look at the feelings that are produced by each person's thoughts. What feelings would be produced by thoughts like, "It's another day, and I get to make money doing what I love to do," or "Wow, I slept really great last night, and I feel amazing"? I think we can all agree that these thoughts would produce feelings of happiness, satisfaction, motivation, etc. What about the thoughts of the other person: "Are you serious — it's already time to get up? I hardly slept at all, and I'm so tired," or "I can't deal with my job when I'm this tired." What feelings are produced by these thoughts? I imagine some of the feelings would be tiredness, defeatedness, sadness, and maybe even some anger. So far, we have the Thing, which is neutral, and we have Realized Thoughts it has caused. Now we have to Understand Feelings that these thoughts have created.

The second T in the T.R.U.T.H. tool stands for "Take Action." The Thing provoked certain thoughts, which in turn created specific feelings. Now we're ready to Take Action based on these feelings. Before we look at the actions in the example we've been using, I want to make sure you understand that our actions are always based on the emotions or feelings we are having. So now let's look at the feelings of the first person, and the action of the person who wakes up thinking about how much they love their job. These thoughts make them feel happy, satisfied, and motivated to get up when the alarm first goes off so that they can be on time for work. What about the second person? They wake up thinking they're too tired to deal with their job today. These thoughts make them feel very tired, defeated, sad, and angry. The actions of this person are to roll over and go back to sleep and not care if they are late for work. So, the Thing has caused each person to Take Action based on the feelings they were having, and these feelings were caused by their individual thoughts about the Thing.

Finally, the H in the T.R.U.T.H. tool is to ask, "How Will This Serve You?" Or, if you are applying the TRUTH tool to something that has already happened, then the H stands for "How Did This Serve You?" The goal is to use the T.R.U.T.H. tool to help you make difficult decisions. But, it is also important to use it to analyze decisions you have already made so you can better understand why you are getting the results you are getting. It will work with positive or negative results. If we recognize something negative that has happened, we can use the T.R.U.T.H. tool to help us figure out why and to then change that result. If something positive has happened, maybe it would be nice to know what we did to get that result so we can keep on getting that result or even make it better. Remember, we can only change our own thoughts, feelings, and actions with the T.R.U.T.H. tool, not anyone else's. So, let's finish with the example we've been using. How do you think the thoughts, feelings, and actions of each person in our scenario will serve them? Can we all agree that the person who is on time for work will likely have a better day at work, please their boss, and accomplish more than the person who is late for work and lacks motivation?

Remember, the T.R.U.T.H. tool will change results if we use it. If you are the person who doesn't like their job and finds it difficult to get up and be on time for work, think about how you can change your thoughts to get a better result (meaning you're on time for work). Maybe look at why you need a job. Some thoughts you could have are "This isn't my dream job, but it's paying my bills and I appreciate that," or "I know I have to work as a condition of my probation/parole, and this job is keeping me from going back to prison." Can you see how changing a simple thought about the exact same circumstance can change your feelings, actions, and end result? That's how powerful our thoughts are.

Let's look at another example of how you could use the T.R.U.T.H. tool. This example is about someone who is reflecting on their childhood. Notice how just one thought can change everything. The comparison on the next page shows how the same circumstance yields different results based on our thoughts, feelings and actions.

TRUTH Tool example

T- the Thing (remember this is neutral)
Dad worked long hours every day and wasn't home very much.
Mom went shopping a lot.

R- Realize thoughts

Thought #1	Thought #2
My dad didn't like spending time with me. He didn't love my mom because she spent all of his money.	My dad worked so hard to make sure we had money for what we needed. My mom always made sure she bought what I needed.

U- Understand Feelings

I'm angry because my parents argued too much and didn't have time for me.	I feel loved because my dad worked so hard for me and my mom made sure I had what I needed.

T- Take Action

Don't spend time with parents.	Spend time with parents

H- How Does That Serve You

I'm depressed and lonely.	I have a great relationship with my parents.

This is just an example and isn't meant to tell you how you should think and feel about your childhood. The T.R.U.T.H. tool is different for every single person and every single circumstance.

You can use the T.R.U.T.H. tool for all situations. On the next pages, there are blank T.R.U.T.H. worksheets. I encourage you to work through these with past situations or with situations you anticipate in the near future. Being able to practice this by working through situations on paper will allow you to turn this into a skill to use for every decision you make.

Chapter Notes & Key Takeaways:

T.R.U.T.H. Worksheet

T — The Thing. Describe the situation:

R — Realize Your Thoughts: Write down your thoughts about the situation:

U — Understand Your Feelings: How do your thoughts about the situation make you feel?:

T — Take Action: What is your action based on your feelings?:

H — How Will This Serve You?: Are the results of your actions positive or negative?:

T.R.U.T.H. Worksheet

T — The Thing. Describe the situation:

R — Realize Your Thoughts: Write down your thoughts about the situation:

U — Understand Your Feelings: How do your thoughts about the situation make you feel?:

T — Take Action: What is your action based on your feelings?:

H — How Will This Serve You?: Are the results of your actions positive or negative?:

Chapter 3

Managing Your Thoughts to Achieve Results

Many people have deep-seated thoughts and feelings that are not productive to their true happiness and that can prevent them from living their best life. This chapter will show how the T.R.U.T.H. tool can be used with any circumstance, no matter how difficult or painful it is.

Guilt and Shame
It's probably safe to assume that each of us knows what guilt feels like. We can feel guilt for something we've done, something we think we've done, or something we didn't get done. If you're in prison, you've probably felt some degree of guilt, whether you are guilty of the crime you're in prison for or not. If you have children, you may feel guilty because you're away from them. Leaving your loved ones may cause feelings of guilt. Maybe you've disappointed someone you care about, and that has caused guilt to build up inside of you. When we hurt another person, especially someone we care about, and we feel sorry about what we did, that can easily move into feelings of guilt.

Guilt and shame are often thought of as the same feeling. If you have a deep feeling of guilt, it is not uncommon to have also felt shame. While guilt and shame may seem similar, there are huge differences between these two feelings. Brené Brown is a research professor and author who has studied the differences between shame and guilt. She describes the difference between shame and guilt like this: "Shame is a focus on self, guilt is a focus on behavior. Shame is, 'I am bad.' Guilt is, 'I did something bad.' How many of you, if you did something that was hurtful to someone you care about, would be willing to say, 'I'm sorry. I made a mistake?'" Another example offered by Brown of the difference in guilt and shame is this: Guilt: "I'm sorry. I made a mistake." Shame: "I'm sorry. I am a mistake."

How easy is it for you to say "I'm sorry" when you realize you've done something that caused hurt to another person? How do you feel before, during, and after apologizing? Do we need to apologize for hurting someone if we were doing what we needed to do and didn't intend to hurt them? I believe we should always apologize when our actions cause another to be hurt or upset. There may be times we have to do something knowing someone we care about will be upset. We can still be sorry that our actions upset them. We can apologize for how our actions made them feel without necessarily apologizing for what we did. How can we know the difference between when our actions directly or indirectly hurt someone? That's where guilt comes in. If someone is feeling hurt as a direct result of our actions, then we will likely feel guilt because of that action and result. If someone is feeling hurt as an indirect result of our action, we will likely not feel any guilt associated with our action. Again, we can and should still acknowledge and even apologize that our actions hurt them.

An example of how actions could directly hurt someone might be when someone gets caught cheating on their spouse. It's easy to imagine how each person feels. The spouse is hurt, upset, and mad. The person who was cheating is likely to feel some guilt. An example of how actions could indirectly hurt someone might be when you have to work late and can't do something that is very important to someone you care about. It's likely you will feel upset or sad because you can't do what your loved one wants you to do, but you shouldn't feel any guilt, because you're doing what you need to do.

Shame is a FEELING, and we can think of it as the thoughts that we are somehow wrong, defective, inadequate, not good enough, or not strong enough. In her research, Brené Brown says this about shame: "Shame is highly, highly correlated with addiction, depression, violence, aggression, bullying, suicide, eating disorders." People with deep feelings of shame are often afraid of what they perceive as their shortcomings or faults being revealed, and this is what leads to these behaviors. Feeling inadequate or like we are not good enough just as we are can cause us to compensate with unwanted or unhealthy behaviors.

While we have all felt shame, most of us don't recognize the varying degrees of shame. Shame can be felt when you fall down in front of a crowd of people. This degree of shame comes on quickly and usually doesn't last very long. It may come and go as those who witnessed your fall remind you of the incident for years to come, but this is mild shame. The most intense degree of shame is humiliation. Humiliation can be so painful that we might have thoughts like, "This is so painful; I wish I could die!"

Are we supposed to try and get rid of guilt and shame? The solution isn't to get rid of them. They are both natural and come with our human relationships. We are human and we're going to do things that hurt others, directly or indirectly. Guilt is a feeling that we can use to guide our behavior. When wondering if what we're about to do will hurt someone else, we can think through it and see if we feel guilt. If we do, we can decide not to do it or to do it differently. If it's too late and we've already done something that has hurt someone, feelings of guilt can guide us to make amends by apologizing for hurting them.

While it might be more comfortable and less painful to cover up our feelings of shame with compensating behaviors, the answer is to do just the opposite. Brené Brown talks about how being vulnerable can help us to overcome shame. Being vulnerable is something a lot of people have fought against their entire lives. Society has taught us that we aren't supposed to let others know when we're feeling anything less than "good." Research now suggests that the path to living our best life is to be real about how we feel. This is easier to do when we have a healthy sense of self-worth.

Self-Worth

What is your self-worth? Is it based on your job, your education, what you have, what you do, how you feel, or maybe a combination of all of these? Some may equate their self-worth to how others view them. Society has determined the social norms around a person's worth, but our sense of self-worth is made up of the thoughts and feelings we believe to be true about ourselves. It's easy to forget that our worth isn't determined by anything outside of us. It comes from within. It's how each of us values our self.

Self-worth is a fundamental feeling that you are worthy as a person. It's not whether others view you as a worthy person. It's based solely on how you view yourself. Self-worth is different that self-esteem. Typically, you must have self-worth before you can have self-esteem. Our self-worth is what lays the foundation for our self-esteem. If we lack self-worth, then it's likely we will also have little or no self-esteem.

So, what causes someone to have low self-worth? There is no clear-cut answer to this. We start developing our sense of worth at a very early age. Our environment and those around us play a part in that. As a toddler I'm sure we were all told "No" or "Bad girl/boy." That seems pretty harmless, right? For most it is probably harmless, but each of us is different in how we develop and cope; therefore, each and every experience we encounter affects us differently. Research has shown that people who experience trauma are more likely to believe there is something fundamentally wrong with them, thus causing low self-worth.

Low self-worth can lead to unhealthy feelings and behaviors. Some of the feelings could be depression, anxiety, stress, and inadequacy. Some unhealthy behaviors might be over-drinking, overeating, self-medicating, or isolation. These unhealthy feelings and behaviors perpetuate the lack of self-worth someone is already feeling. There are thousands of self-help books that examine and explain self-worth in much more detail. Also, talking to a professional and getting guidance is a good way to overcome low self-worth.

Every single person is worthy. We are all worthy of goodness, love, and acceptance. Oftentimes it is our fear that convinces us we're not — fear of what others will think of us and fear of what might happen if we live our true and authentic life.

Marianne Williamson famously put it this way:

Our deepest fear is not that we are inadequate. Our deepest fear is that we are powerful beyond measure. It is our light, not our darkness, that most frightens us. We ask ourselves, "Who am I to be brilliant, gorgeous, talented, and fabulous?" Actually, who are you not to be? You are a child of God. Your playing small does not serve the world. There is nothing enlightened about shrinking so that other people will not feel insecure around you. We are all meant to shine, as children do.

Trauma

Looking back on our lives, we've all made decisions that we can now see weren't the best for us. Have you ever wondered why some people do the things they do? Why do we do things that obviously aren't healthy or in our best interest or the interest of those we care about? Every single person has what is called *free will*. This means that we have the ability to choose one thing over another. We have the ability to discern what we should and shouldn't do. Some may ask, why would anyone ever choose to hurt themselves or those around them? This question is not easy to answer, as there are many reasons we do the things we do. Each and every life experience from birth until now has influenced our decisions and brought us to where we are today.

There has been much research on how trauma directly affects decisions we make. Trauma is a deeply disturbing or painful event that surpasses our ability to cope. In simple terms, it is when something horrible happens that we have no control over. Trauma can cause us to feel overwhelmed, anxious, helpless, scared, and numb. Trauma can be acute, meaning it's short lived, or it can be chronic, meaning it remains for some time. Repeated trauma over a period of time may cause severe psychological conditions.

It is difficult to understand the extent our life is affected by trauma because trauma is so hard to process. However, realizing you have experienced trauma is the first step in being able to heal from it. Once you come to terms with the fact that something negative and out of your control happened, you can start looking at the thoughts, feelings and actions you are having in relation to the trauma. You will learn about several self-coaching practices in this book that can help you process and heal from trauma, but depending on the degree of the trauma you experienced, you may need to talk to a professional to start the healing process.

<u>Chapter Notes & Key Takeaways:</u>

-

Using the T.R.U.T.H. Tool to Overcome Guilt

T — The Thing: I have feelings of guilt because ...:

R — Realize Thoughts: Is this guilt directly (productive) or indirectly (nonproductive) related to something I did or didn't do that was within my control? (Describe.)

U — Understand Feelings: What feelings are this guilt causing me to have?

T — Take action: Do I need to apologize to anyone? If yes, to whom, and what will I say?

H — How will/did this serve me?

You can use this process as many times as necessary to address situations that are causing you feelings of guilt.

Using the T.R.U.T.H. Tool to Overcome Shame

T — The Thing: What is happening as a result of feeling shame?
    (An example might be "I avoid my parents.")

R — Realize Thoughts: What thoughts am I having about what I wrote in #1? (From the example, what are the thoughts that are making you avoid your parents?)

U — Understand Feelings: Based on the thoughts I wrote, what feelings am I having? (One of the feelings should be shame, but there could be more.)

T— Take action: What should or could I do in this moment to feel better and work
    towards releasing the feeling of shame?

H — How will/did this serve me?

You can use this process as many times as necessary to address situations that are causing you feelings of shame.

Using the T.R.U.T.H. Tool to Overcome Trauma

T — The Thing: What is the negative experience?

R — Realize Thoughts: What thoughts am I having about what I wrote in #1?

U — Understand Feelings: Based on the thoughts I wrote, what feelings am I having?

T — Take action: What action(s) am I taking based on these feelings?

H — How will/did this serve me?

You can use this process as many times as necessary to address different thoughts and feelings related to trauma.

Chapter 4

Tools for Self-Coaching

Self-coaching means just that: You are coaching yourself. Most of us have had a coach or mentor at some point in our life who gave us advice or taught us how to do something. With self-coaching, you are the one giving the advice. This advice is based on your thoughts and feelings about any situation. Remember the T.R.U.T.H. tool and how we can use it to help us make changes to get results that serve us? This is one tool we can use to self-coach. There are other self-coaching tools that you might also find useful.

Thought Download

Does your mind ever seem so full of thoughts, ideas, and to-do's that you don't know where or how to get started? This can cause worry, stress, and anxiety. Would you like to change some of your thoughts and decrease your stress level? A practice known as a *Thought Download* can help. This is simply putting all your thoughts on paper. The goal is to put your thoughts on paper so you can examine them and determine which ones are true and which ones are not, and ultimately decrease stress a thought may be causing. Essentially you will be eavesdropping on yourself so you can learn how to think new thoughts. Once you've written down all your thoughts, separate your thoughts from facts. For example, if your parents are coming to visit and you haven't seen them in a long time, your Thought Download list could include the following: 1. My parents are coming to visit, 2. I've disappointed them. When you separate these two statements into thoughts and facts, you'll easily see that number one is a fact and number two is a thought. Once you have identified your thoughts, use the T.R.U.T.H. tool to work through each one. Doing this will allow you to determine the thoughts that aren't serving you so you can change them.

When doing a Thought Download, you should try to keep writing for 5-10 minutes. Here are some questions you can ask yourself to help prompt your thoughts.

1. What do you wish were different?
2. What is hurting or frustrating you?
3. What are you struggling with?
4. What are you worried about?
5. What doubts do you have about reaching your goals?
6. What are your priorities today or this week?

Here's another example of how writing down our thoughts and feelings may help us. Have you ever been upset or angry with someone, and instead of speaking to them face to face, you decided to sit down and write them a letter telling them how you feel? If you have done this, I am going to bet you felt better after writing the letter before you even gave it to them. Putting our thoughts and feelings on paper gets them out of our head and lessens the degree to which we were feeling hurt, disappointed, angry, etc. I'm not saying it's always good to write down our feelings and never have those hard, face-to-face conversations. What I am saying is that writing down our thoughts and feelings is a powerful tool that we can use when we want to think or feel better or when we want to increase our self-awareness.

Next, we'll look at how to do a Thought Download with our to-do lists and goals. Begin by writing down everything you would like to get done in the next month. Next, prioritize them in the order you want to do them. Some tasks may take several steps to complete. You can write down each of these steps as part of your to-do list. Now, write each task and step on your calendar. Simple, right? Here's the challenge: Now you must honor yourself by honoring what you have written on your calendar. If one of your to-do items is to read a self-help book and you put on your calendar to read for an hour every Tuesday, then you must read for an hour every Tuesday. The awesome thing about doing this is that all of those to-do's and goals are out of your head and on your calendar, which means the worry, stress, and anxiety about when you're going to do them is out of your head as well. This is a great tool to have in your self-coaching toolbox.

Use this exercise to help you understand how the thought download exercise works. This worksheet is based on the T.R.U.T.H. tool and provides a step-by-step process for doing a thought download. I encourage you to complete this worksheet in order to better understand the process. You can do this exercise using a goal or things you need to get done.

T — The Thing: Example: I have so many things I need to get done.
Write your specific Thing.

R — Realize Thoughts: Write down your thoughts associated with how this makes you feel. Example: There's no way I can get all this done in time.

U — Understand Feelings: Write down the feelings that your thoughts are creating for you. Example: I'm feeling overwhelmed and discouraged.

T — Take Action: What action should you take based on the thoughts and feelings you wrote above? This is where you can write down all your tasks or goal steps and then prioritize in the order you want to do them. After you do this, put them on your calendar.

H — How will/did this serve me? What will change for the better by doing this? Example: I no longer have to stress about when I'm going to do specific tasks.

Journaling

Journaling is a very common practice that many people do when they desire to change or to grow within a specific aspect of their life. Writing down everyday experiences helps us to recognize what worked for us and what worked against us throughout our day. This is one of the simplest tools we can add into our daily routine. This simple tool can improve your life beyond what you can imagine. It is life changing.

There are many areas of our lives where we can use journaling. Some may choose to have just one journal and write everything down in one place. Others might find it better to have a different journal for different areas of their life. For instance, maybe you prefer to have a journal about work and a different journal about relationships. It really doesn't matter how you journal as long as you do it. This practice will allow you to examine every aspect of your life. You will begin to recognize what you really want and need in order to live your best life.

A "Gratitude Journal" is a common journal that many people have. If you've never done a gratitude journal, I highly recommend trying it. At the end of each day you simply think of three to five things you are grateful for and write them in your journal. Of course, if you are grateful for more than five things in your day, you can write them all down. The key is to write down at least three to five. This is an easy practice when everything is going great, so the challenge comes when you're in a low period or dark period in your life. When you practice journaling regularly, you will see that even in those times, there are things to be grateful for. You may have to think longer and harder to recognize them, but don't give up, because I promise you will think of them.

The benefits of keeping a gratitude journal go beyond just helping us realize what we're grateful for each and every day. Once we've written down what we're grateful for, the next step is to actually feel gratitude towards each of those things. When we can truly feel gratitude for all the good around us, we will soon recognize that more and more things to be grateful for are showing up in our lives.

Journaling

First, decide if your journal will be about your life in general or if it will be specific to one area of your life: gratitude, health, project, diet, family, goals, travel, career, spiritual, etc.

Here are some questions to get you started. Just think about the answers; choosing a topic to journal about will come next:

1. What was the best thing about today?
2. What made me smile today?
3. What made me feel stress today?
4. How did I help someone today?
5. How did someone help me today?
6. What did I learn today?
7. How was I productive at work today?
8. What self-care did I do today?
9. Did I make healthy food choices today?
10. What did I do today to develop my personal/spiritual growth?

What topic of your life will you start journaling about today?

I chose this topic of my life to journal about because

How often will you write in your journal?

How long will you keep journaling on this topic?

Once you commit to yourself to journal, it's important to do it as often and for as long as you stated you would. You honor yourself by following through with decisions you make. Most agree, once you get in the habit of journaling it becomes a lifelong practice.

Meditation

Meditation is a technique for quieting the mind and moving into a deeper state of consciousness or awareness. For some it is a spiritual practice, and for some it's simply a way to uncloud their mind and gain clarity and focus. It doesn't matter the reason why; those who have a daily practice of meditation find it extremely beneficial. My hope is that you will at least give it a try.

For most of us, it's a difficult practice when we first begin. Have you ever tried to clear your mind of all thoughts? Our minds are meant to think, right? Most of us can think hundreds of random thoughts in as little as a minute or two. It seems nearly impossible to clear our minds of all these thoughts. Not to worry — many long-time meditators still report random thoughts entering and leaving their minds while meditating. The key is to let the thoughts leave and become an observer.

If you're willing to give it a try, I'll share how I got started and how my habit has developed over the years. For me, meditation is a spiritual practice. But, like I said before, there are many reasons people meditate. The reasons do not matter because the goal is the same: to get to the same place of a quiet mind and deeper consciousness. For me, it's important to be in a comfortable, sitting position. I prefer a chair, but others prefer sitting on the floor or lying down. There is no right or wrong way as long as you're comfortable. Another consideration is whether to meditate in complete silence or to have soft music playing. This is a personal preference. For me, I liked music or guided meditations in the beginning, and now I'm more comfortable in complete silence.

Once I'm comfortable and in a quiet place, I like to take several deep breaths, in through my nose and out through my mouth. This helps me to relax. If I need more help relaxing, I start with my head and relax each muscle all the way to my toes. It's important to actually feel each muscle relax as you do this. Once I'm completely relaxed, I begin to focus on my breathing. This helps me to not think about anything else. Random thoughts may enter my mind, but I regain focus on my breathing and let the thoughts leave. When I first started my meditation practice, this cycle of breathing and random thoughts lasted a long time, sometimes throughout my entire meditation time. The key is to continue practicing. You will notice that the random thoughts become fewer and fewer and you are able to quiet your mind more easily.

I can't stress enough that there is no right or wrong way to meditate. It's all about quieting the mind long enough to feel connected to something beyond our normal experience. For some this may be sitting quietly in nature or along a river listening to the water flow. For others it means being immersed in something they absolutely love doing. Wanting to achieve feelings of pure love and joy are excellent reasons to meditate. If you're new to mediation and would like to learn more, I encourage you to find a book about meditation practices or talk to someone who currently has a meditation practice.

Here are some common types of meditation:

Mindfulness meditation. Mindfulness meditation originates from Buddhist teachings and is the most popular meditation technique in the West. This type of meditation is good for people who don't have a teacher to guide them, as it can be easily practiced alone.

Spiritual meditation. Used in Eastern religions, such as Hinduism and Daoism, as well as in the Christian faith, this form of meditation is similar to prayer in that you reflect on the silence around you and seek a deeper connection with your God or Universe. This practice is beneficial for those who thrive in silence and seek spiritual growth.

Focused meditation. Focused meditation involves concentration using any of the five senses. This practice is ideal for anyone who desires additional focus in their life.

Movement meditation. This variety of meditation may include walking in nature, gardening, or other gentle forms of movement. This type is good for those who find peace in action and prefer to let their minds wander.

Mantra meditation. This form of meditation uses a repetitive sound to clear the mind. A mantra can be a word, phrase, or sound. Some people like this method because they find it easy to focus on a word and enjoy repetition.

Transcendental Meditation. This trademarked method is the most popular and most scientifically studied around the world. This practice is for those who like structure and are serious about maintaining a meditation practice.

Steps to Begin a Meditation Practice

1. Find a quiet place to do this. If it isn't possible to find a completely quiet place, then choose somewhere with as few noises and distractions as possible. The best place for me to meditate is _____.

2, Get in a comfortable position. This can be sitting on a chair or on the floor or lying down.

3. Once you're comfortable, you can either close your eyes or keep your eyes open and focused on a particular object.

4. Take 2-3 deep breaths, each in through your nose and exhaled through your mouth.

5. Move through your body and relax every muscle. Notice parts of your body where there is tension or pain, and feel it release as you relax.

6. You can focus your meditation on a specific topic or area of your life, or you may prefer to simply quiet your mind and focus on your breathing.

7. As random thoughts enter your mind, gently notice them and let them go.

8. If you have limited time for this, you may want to set a timer.

9. Practice this as often as you want.

10. Develop a schedule and stay committed.

Are you willing to give meditation a try? If so, when will you start? _____

How many minutes a day will you meditate? _____

How many times a week will you mediate? _____

Remember, quieting or stillness of mind is the most common goal of meditation. Including the practice above, there are many ways to accomplish a quiet, still mind. Some of these ways are exercise, nature, music, rest, animals, pictures, yoga, creating, gardening, and many others.

Personal Growth/Continuous Learning

A lifelong goal for each of us might be to continually learn and grow as a person. This lifelong goal is called personal growth or personal development. We should never stop wanting to better ourselves. John C. Maxwell is a well-known leadership and personal growth author and one of my favorites on this topic. His book, *The 15 Invaluable Laws of Growth*, is a great book to show us how we can grow in different areas of our lives. This book was my first glimpse into why personal growth and development are so important. We must remember that there is no finish line. We are never done. Continuous learning and personal growth are key to us living our best life. I have included a list of popular personal growth books at the end of this chapter.

Something as simple as reading ten pages of a self-help book a day can keep you on a personal growth path. Taking classes and participating in groups are other ways to continue learning and growing. There is more information readily available to us than there ever has been before, through the internet, TV, books, social media, etc. Having access to information is never an issue. However, it's not enough to read and know how to improve. We must apply what we read and hear to our lives for the growth to actually take place. Remember, it's not enough just to know it; we have to apply it. That is when the real change and growth happens.

For instance, I can read all the diet and exercise books I can get my hands on, but if I never change the way I eat or exercise, I'm not going to lose any weight. Simply knowing the information does not change my circumstances. It's the action of applying the knowledge that changes circumstances. I think this is important to realize. I may feel like I'm doing some real personal growth by reading all about what I need to eat and how I need to exercise, but that's only the first step. Educating ourselves is an important first step in reaching our goals, but it's the action we take after we learn that gets us to our goal.

While on your personal growth path, there are some things you can do that will help keep you on course. First, it's important to surround yourself with supportive people. These are people who want to see you succeed and want all your dreams to come true. These are your people. Your people are for you and your best life. Next, learn about and have access to as many supportive resources as you possibly can. This may be your favorite self-help book, a counselor, a minister, or any other support that will help you stay on your personal growth path. Things will happen that will test your ability to stay focused on your dreams, and that is why having supportive people and supportive resources at your fingertips is so important.

The last practice I want to mention that will help you stay on your personal growth path is goal setting. Think about your dreams and what you desire. No matter how big and impossible you think they seem right now, setting goals can keep you moving in the direction of your dreams. Ask yourself what you want your life to look like in ten years or even five years. Then, think of what smaller steps you can take that will get you closer to that. It's important that your goals are specific and achievable. Set a timeframe for each goal so you stay on track. Reaching goals, no matter how small they are, builds confidence and motivates us to keep moving forward.

Personal Growth and Development Tips

Introduce you to you. Study yourself and learn who you really are. Have you conformed to the expectations and standards of others, or are you living authentically to who you truly are?

Stretch beyond your typical limits and get out of your comfort zone. That is when true growth occurs. If we do what we always do because we know we can do it, we will not experience growth. You must step into new areas in order to grow.

Be OK if others judge you or put you down. It's really none of your business what someone else thinks of you; it's theirs. You have to accept that you will not please all the people all the time. It's not your job to please others. Your focus should be on how to be the best version of yourself.

Learn how to be assertive when necessary. You have to stand up for yourself and your needs. Nothing good ever comes from holding back feelings until you explode. It's best to express yourself as feelings happen and avoid the explosion. Make your feelings a priority.

Start one or all of the self-coaching practices you've read about in this chapter. There are many other personal growth practices you can develop in addition to these.

Develop your action plan. State your personal growth goals, such as books you want to read, exercises you want to do, conversations you want to have, classes you want to take, etc. Once you know what you want to do, develop a schedule to get started and reach your goals.

Maintain a positive attitude. It's no secret that a positive attitude serves us much better than a negative one. Something simple to remember is that positivity attracts positivity and negativity attracts negativity.

Be grateful. No matter where you are or what is going on in your life, there are things to be grateful for. Never lose sight of this. When you start identifying things in your life that you're grateful for, more things to be grateful for will start showing up.

Learn how to do new things. Start a new hobby or learn a new craft. Start a new job that you've never done before. No matter your current situation, there are opportunities for you to learn new things.

Focus on happiness. Life is too short to focus on misery or discontent. Each minute that passes is gone forever. If we're not paying attention, each new minute will build from the previous. The beautiful thing is that, in any moment of every day, we can decide to change our thoughts and attitude.

Visioning Future Life/Self

Do you have a vision for your life? Maybe you've never thought much about it. If you haven't, then I would ask, do you have hopes and dreams? A vision, a dream, and what we hope for are all concepts about what we desire. I like to think of a vision as something that encompasses all our dreams, hopes, and desires into one big picture. To better explain this, I am going to share with you what a vision board is and why this could be a helpful tool.

Did you know you have the ability to shape your life using your imagination? If you already know this, my hope is you can use this vision board tool to sharpen or update your vision. If this is all new to you, my hope is that you will be open to giving this tool a try. I hope you will better understand how you can use the power of visioning to create the life only you can imagine.

When we accomplish a desire, fulfill a goal, or get to that next level, we increase our awareness and vibrations around what we've accomplished. We feel happiness, joy, and a sense of well-being. When we are in that space, we feel in tune with our best self. This is also when we have the highest capacity to give of ourselves to others. Spending time to intentionally create a vision just helps ensure we get closer to our desired destination.

A vision board is a tool that can help you clarify and focus on goals that lead to your best life. This is often done by creating a collage of images or words that represent who you want to be, what you want to do, or things you would like to have. It's really just about setting a goal for yourself and giving your brain a picture of what that might look like. We do this all the time without thinking about it. A common thought that many of us have had is the thought that we need to lose weight. Most of us start with, "I want to lose weight," and then we might refine it to, "I want to lose 20 pounds." We might also start to think of it in terms of what size clothing we want to be able to wear when we reach our goal or how we want to feel in a swimming suit. As we start to think about or envision those outcomes of losing weight, it becomes easier to turn down that double-fudge brownie because it doesn't fit with the vision we have created.

The first step is to get clearer about what area of your life you want your vision board to focus on. It is helpful to break down life into eight major categories. You can create a vision board that covers one, two, or all of them combined. The categories are family and friends, significant other, health, personal growth, career, fun and leisure, home environment, and money. A good way to begin this process is to decide how satisfied you currently are in each of the categories. Try to list them in order from least satisfied to most satisfied. Once you have them prioritized, choose one of the areas you are least satisfied in and would like to improve.

Once you've decided what you want to focus your vision board on, think about what would improve that area of your life to move it towards the satisfied list. If it helps, you can write down your thoughts about how you'd like to improve this area of your life. If you do this, you may already begin to feel your mood lift a little just thinking about how your life would look with these improvements.

Now that you've decided which area(s) to focus on for your vision board, it's time to create. Remember, there is no right or wrong way to create your vision board; it can be whatever you need it to be to help you focus on your desires. Simply find words or pictures that symbolize what you want. You can write them, draw them on your board, or, if you have access to magazines, you can find words and pictures to cut out and glue on your board. Some people like to print words and pictures off the internet. It doesn't matter how the objects get on your vision board. The purpose is to have something that you look at or read daily as a reminder of the vision and goals you want to achieve.

There are other tools, such as a visioning worksheet, that are also great ways to help you create a vision. This worksheet uses the eight life categories previously mentioned. The goal of a vision statement is to write out your goals in language that indicates those actions have already taken place. For example, in our weight-loss scenario from earlier, we might say, "I show I am focused on taking care of my health by eating healthy foods. I have the energy to complete the tasks I need to each day with plenty left over to enjoy my favorite outdoor activities." The visioning worksheet will help you realize what you truly desire in your life.

Another fun activity is to visualize what you want your life to be like in five years. Really think about where you will be, what you will be doing, how you will feel etc. You do this with any of the eight life categories. Then pretend you just ran into someone you haven't seen in that five years. Write down all the things you would have to tell them to catch them up on your life.

Visioning Statement Worksheet

Really think about the life only you can imagine for yourself. What actions will allow you to reach that vision? Create a personal vision statement in language that indicates those actions have already taken place. When your mind can see it, you can BE it!

I am committed to living my best life. It feels so good to take care of myself in a way that allows me to be more available to the people and activities that are important to me.

I show I am focused on improving my health by:

My relationships with others are stronger because I:

I am open to opportunities for personal growth including:

I value fun and time to relax by:

My living space is a place of peace and renewal because I:

I am improving my career opportunities by:

Financial freedom is in my reach because I am:

The 5 Year Life Visualization

1. Write down your vision for how your life will be five years from now. This vision can be specific to one area of your life, such as job or family, or it can be broader to cover all areas of your life. It's up to you.

2. At this five-year mark, imagine running in to an old friend and the two of you sitting down and catching up on what's been going on within each other's lives.

3. Now, focus on and write down all the things you've experienced over this time frame that have led you to the amazing life you're living now.

4. Notice how it makes you feel when you visualize and focus on living the life you dream of. Write down a couple of the most noticeable feelings you had while doing this exercise.

Your Purpose

Have you discovered your purpose? We all have one. If you know your true purpose, then you are one of the fortunate few. If you know your purpose, then hopefully you are taking steps to live and achieve it. Sometimes I think about how awesome it would be if we were born knowing our purpose and could confidently proceed without question, but we all know that isn't the case. There is something mysterious and exciting about coming into and discovering our individual purpose. Some people know their purpose early on, and their life is driven by that. Others may not discover their purpose until later in life. Some may think they know their purpose and begin to fulfill their desires, and doing so leads them on a path to their true purpose. Our experiences guide us and can help us discover our purpose.

The self-coaching tools I've mentioned in this book are all great ways to gain focus and clarity on what your true desires are for your life. We all want to be the best version of ourselves and live out our individual hopes and dreams. Once we are on a path of self-improvement and self-discovery, oftentimes our purpose will be revealed to us. Please don't get discouraged if you feel like you should be doing something but don't know exactly what that something is or how to accomplish it. Just keep doing the next thing that is true and right for you, and you'll be well on your way to achieving your desires.

It's important to find joy in the journey to discovering your purpose. Even if you feel your true purpose will never be revealed to you, I encourage you to examine what you have accomplished while on your self-discovery journey. Doing what feels right and true to who you are will keep you on the path of living your best life. I believe that for each of us, part of our purpose *is* to live our best life.

Chapter Notes & Key Takeaways:

Part 2: Life After Incarceration

The first part of this book is all about helping you become more aware of how situations or things create thoughts, which create feelings, which cause action, which finally gives us our results. If you understand and believe this process, then you now realize that you are in complete control of your life. If you understand and believe this, it will change your life.

Part 2 of this book will focus on practical things that we all need to survive day to day, from our basic needs being met, to a source of income, to a good support system. We all have the same basic needs and desires that help us exist in the world. Just because you are in prison does not mean you don't have needs and desires or that your basic needs changed automatically when you walked through the prison doors.

The rest of this book will give you some great information that you can use now, while in prison, to help better prepare yourself for life after incarceration. My sincere hope is that the information in this book, Part 1 and Part 2, gives you the knowledge and motivation to take control of your life while you are in prison. I hope you will realize that you are the only person who truly has control over your life.

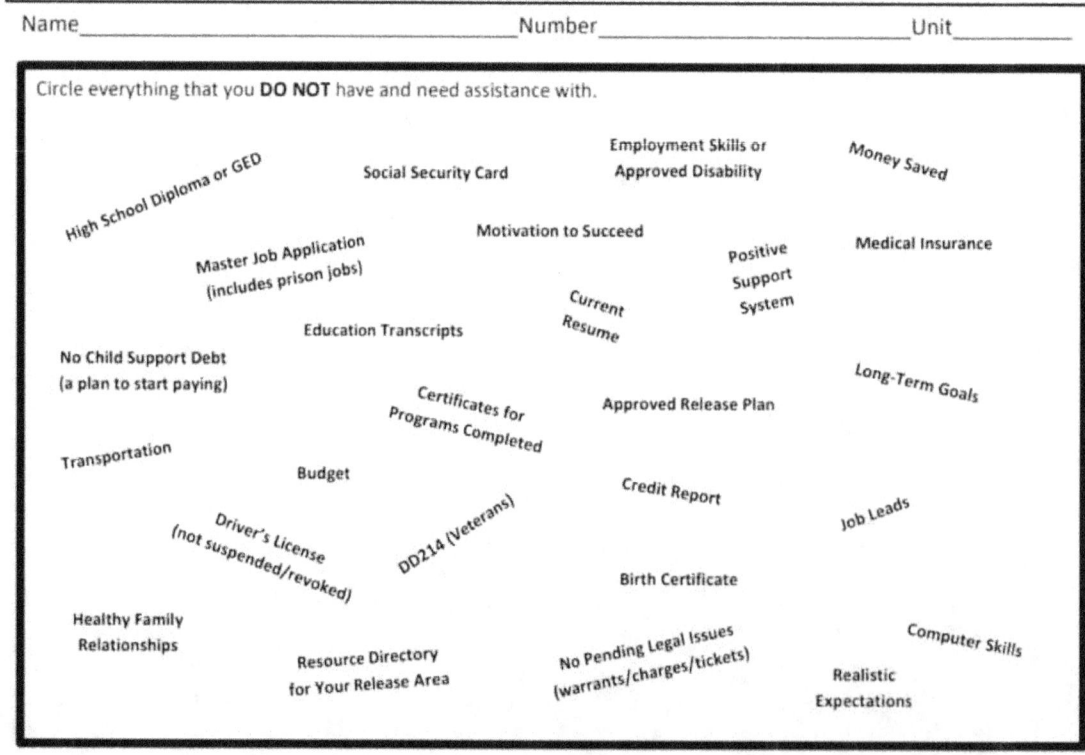

Chapter 5

Abundance & Basic Needs: Housing, Food, Finances

Abundance & Prosperity
"Today expect something good to happen to you no matter what occurred yesterday. Realize the past no longer holds you captive. It can only continue to hurt you if you hold on to it. Let the past go. A simply abundant world awaits." — Sarah Breathnach

Do you know that you already have everything you need to be successful? You have everything you need to create the exact life you desire. Stop and think about that for a minute. You might be thinking, "But I need more money," or, "I don't have _____" (you fill in the blank). Maybe you're waiting for this to happen or that to happen before you can be truly satisfied. If objects, jobs, or money (all things outside of us) were all we needed to be happy and successful, then how is it that some people seem to have all those things and are still unhappy? The secret is to first be happy with who you are. Take away all the outside distractions and focus on *you*. That is where true happiness begins. Once we realize this and find our true happiness in just being who we are, everything else adds to this. If happiness is not found in who we are, we can add all the treasures of the world to our lives and still not be happy.

Have you heard of the Law of Attraction? This universal law simply states that we have the ability to attract into our lives whatever we are focusing on. This law works in both directions. If you are focused on negative, depressing things, those are the things you will continue to attract. But, if you focus on positive, happy thoughts, you will attract just that: positivity and happiness. That sounds easy, doesn't it? Just change your thoughts to all good, and all good is what you will attract. This might be possible if you lived in an environment where every single thing around you was good and happy. For most, that is not the case. It definitely takes practice and a training of the mind to stay focused on the good we want in our lives. This may mean we spend a good portion of our day redirecting our mind back to what we want to focus on. One encounter with an angry person could derail us and send our thoughts spiraling out of control. The goal is to recover quickly from these moments and return our thoughts to what we desire. With practice, you will find that although some encounters or circumstances may cause undesirable thoughts and feelings, you will be able to dismiss them easily and quickly and return your focus to the life you desire.

So how does this Law of Attraction really work? Well, it starts with a thought. Thoughts are powerful because they produce feelings and emotions. Think about something you want, and then *feel* how it would feel to have it. The Law of Attraction is already in motion. Once you have allowed your feelings to emerge from that thought, your actions will line up with those feelings, and you will begin attracting things into your life that support what you desire. For example, let's say you wish you had continued your education after high school. You think about a job you would love to do and how much more money you could make to support yourself and your family. Use your imagination to see yourself exceling in that job. How does that make you feel? Those good thoughts and feelings will begin attracting circumstances, people, and things into your life to assist you in achieving your desire. Your actions also come into play. Maybe you decide to enroll in one class, and in that class, you meet a teacher or another student who inspires you. Maybe you finish that class and immediately want to take another. When your thoughts, feelings, and actions are aligned and focused on what you want, everything else just seems to fall into place. This is the Law of Attraction.

Basic Needs

There are basic needs that, when met, allow us to live a more comfortable life. We all need a place to live, food to eat, and money to sustain us. We cannot ignore the fact that there are plenty of people living among us who do not have one, or all, of these things. But, if you want to thrive, and not just survive, have a plan on now you will make sure your basic needs are met once you release.

Housing

Where you choose to live when you release from prison will be an important step towards your success. Your environment will either encourage you to stay on your positive path of success or it will distract you from your goals and cause you to work much harder to stay on your positive path. Your environment cannot be the sole cause of your success or your failure, but the people, places, and things around you either build into the life you desire or they do not. The important thing here is to recognize the difference and adjust accordingly. When you initially leave prison, you might not have any control over your environment. You might be releasing to an environment that will challenge the very thing you want most — not to go back to prison. Your thought processes and decision-making ability will be tested again and again. Remember, your thoughts create your feelings, which drive your actions, ultimately leading to your results. Keep your mind focused on your dreams and goals. Always ask yourself, *does this support the life I'm trying to create?*

One housing option that many people choose to release to is a halfway house or transitional housing facility. Transitional housing facilities are a great option if you need extra support and a little time to get on your feet after release. Staff at these facilities will have knowledge of resources and programs in your community. These facilities will also meet several basic needs, such as housing and food, and some may offer access to clothing. The challenging aspect of transitional housing is that everyone living there is in the same boat as you. They are either reentering society from incarceration or they are there because something in their life has gone wrong. Unfortunately, not everyone residing at the facility will be in the same positive frame of mind that you're in. You might find yourself being tempted to revert back to some of the old behaviors that led you to prison in the first place. Before you release and before you are faced with a scenario that could jeopardize your freedom again, think about how you would react in that situation. Think about how you would feel and how you would react. What would you say to someone asking you to join them in something you know does not support the life you are trying to create? Thinking through and preparing for these challenging situations now will make it easier for you to react in a way that supports the life you desire.

Another housing option when you release might be living with a family member until you can get your own place. This could be your parents, grandparents, siblings, aunts, or uncles. It doesn't really matter how the person is related to you; the real factor here is how they will (or will not) support your goals. What type of influence will your family member have on what you are trying to accomplish? Remember to do your T.R.U.T.H. work when making these important decisions. Living with family has definite benefits. Typically, they love you and want to see you succeed. They don't mind helping you out for a few weeks or months until you can get on your feet. They have food, shelter, transportation, and maybe even some clothing to help get you started. So what's the catch? While you're in prison, everyone else's life keeps going, without you physically there. They miss you and wish you were there, but they figure out how to get by without you. They have to. Something you will have to realize and accept is that when you release from prison to a family member's home, you instantly become more work for them. Unless you are one of the few who saved enough money while in prison to support yourself for three to six months after release, you may be a financial burden to your family member. This may sound harsh, but it's meant to get you thinking now about what you need to do so that you are not as much of a burden as you would be if you put no thought into it. Your family member may not think of you as a burden and most certainly would never say those words out loud. But, if they are buying extra food, taking you to your appointments, doing extra laundry, etc., it won't take long before they will need to see some progress on your part to keep them motivated to continue helping you.

It becomes a real give-and-take relationship. Your family will give help and are happy to do so. You will take their help because you just got out of prison and don't have a lot of options. Now it's your turn to give something, and all they want from you is to see that you are making the next right decision and doing what you have to do to stay out of prison. They'll gladly take you making right decisions in exchange for their continued support. Do you see the pattern? One of the best ways to repair relationships with those who love you is to simply make progress. Your progress will be determined by the simple, everyday decisions you make. You may have a clear path in your mind leading to a fresh, free life. Remember, though, that your family can't see inside your mind. They can only see behavior. You may become discouraged or even frustrated if your mom or dad repeatedly asks you, "Where are you going?" or, "How long are you going to be?" or, "Where were you?" After all, you are a grown adult. You know what you are doing, and you know you're making good decisions to better your life. So, how can you get those around you to relax and believe in you? The answer is in your actions. When they see you doing the next right thing, day after day, they will relax. They will begin to trust that you are doing everything you need to do to ensure you never go back to prison. This doesn't mean you can't or won't make mistakes. Everyone makes mistakes, not just those who have been to prison. If you make a mistake, recognize it as just that — a mistake. It doesn't mean anything more than that. A lot of people look at mistakes as opportunities to grow and learn. As long as you can see the lessons in your mistakes, you can move forward, not just from them but because of them.

T.R.U.T.H. work example:

T — The Thing is that you are working on your home plan. You know could go back to your mom's house, or you could instead release to your aunt's house. R — Recognize your thoughts associated with each of these options. Mom has always been supportive, and you know she loves you. And you also know she has rules that she'll expect you to follow. Your aunt was there for you when you were involved in the illegal actions that landed you in prison. She's always been supportive, too, but in a very different way than Mom. Your aunt would allow some things that you know your mom wouldn't. U — Understand how you're feeling as you process these thoughts. Maybe you feel safer and more relaxed at your mom's house because you know she would build into the life you want to create. But at your aunt's house, you feel more independent and will be able to do whatever you want. You also feel more anxiety about that because being more independent means doing more for yourself and having less support. T — Think about the actions you would take in each scenario. Based on your thoughts and feelings, which option do you choose? H — How does that option serve you and the life you desire?

Food, Clothing, Transportation

Finding supportive housing after release is a big relief. Once that is done, you can focus on other things you will need. For example, you will need food, clothing, and transportation. Depending on your housing situation, food may be provided. If it is, that's one less thing you have to think about. If it is not, you will need to find resources that can assist you. One option might be visiting the local Division of Family Support

(DFS) office and seeing if you qualify for assistance with food. If you qualify, then this resource will provide financial assistance to purchase food. Another option is a food bank. Most, if not all, communities have a food bank. Typically, you will need identification and proof of income to qualify to receive food at a food bank. Faith-based organizations are another option to consider. Some churches have their own food banks. And, churches typically have the leeway to help individuals on a case-by-case basis. So, depending on what you're needing help with, reaching out to your local churches might be a good option.

One of the biggest barriers a lot of people releasing from prison face is transportation, especially if you are going to be on probation or parole after release, because you will have court-ordered obligations you must meet. If you're releasing in a bigger city, public transportation will be an option for you. All you will have to think about is getting bus tickets. Many towns do not have public transportation, or maybe they just have one bus line and it takes hours to get across town. If that's the case, you won't be able to rely on public transportation. Taxis are an option, but this could get expensive if it's your only way to get around. Other companies like Uber and Lift offer rides at a little cheaper rate than taxis. Owning a vehicle comes with expenses that many can't afford immediately after release. Outside of walking or riding a bicycle, asking friends and family for rides may be your only option when you first release. Discuss this with your family and friends before you release. Asking them for help with transportation before you release doesn't just give them time to prepare to help you; it will also let them know that you're thinking about your future.

Most communities have recognized the need to have resources and support programs for people coming out of prison. And, most have put this information in a community resource guide that can be found and printed from the internet. It's important to learn about what is available in your community before you release from prison. If the prison has someone who will work with you on release preparation, ask them if there is a resource guide for your community, and ask if they will print it out for you. If you can't get a copy this way, then ask someone at home if they will mail a copy to you. If that doesn't work either, you can attempt to get a copy by writing the Chamber of Commerce in your community and asking for a copy. Once you have a copy, you can begin writing the organizations and asking about their programs and resources. Resources are there and willing to help, but you have to reach out to them. They can't help you if they don't know you need help. Doing some pre-release work to help ensure your basic needs are met will allow you to focus your attention on other areas of your life when you do leave prison.

Some of the most important work you can do to prepare for your release is identify ahead of time your potential barriers and create a plan of action to overcome each. Use the chart below to identify common barriers. Keep in mind that you may have barriers specific to your situation that are not listed in this chart. You can write them in the blank spaces at the bottom. Use the next pages to work through each barrier you said yes to and identify community resources and possible solutions.

Potential Barrier	Is this a barrier for me? Yes or No	Will I need help to overcome this barrier? Yes or No
Housing		
Food		
Transportation		
Substance Abuse		
Clothing		
Employment		
Medical Care		
Support System		
Low or No Income		
Family Issues		
Child Support		
Driver's License		
Pending Legal Issue		

Barrier: _____

Possible solutions:

1. _____

2. _____

3. _____

List resources in your release community that offers assistance with this barrier:

	Name of agency or program	Contact person and phone number	Mailing address	Date I sent letter to request information.
1				
2				
3				
4				
5				

Barrier: _____

Possible solutions:

1. _____

2. _____

3. _____

List resources in your release community that offers assistance with this barrier:

	Name of agency or program	Contact person and phone number	Mailing address	Date I sent letter to request information.
1				
2				
3				
4				
5				

Barrier: _____

Possible solutions:

1. _____

2. _____

3. _____

List resources in your release community that offers assistance with this barrier:

	Name of agency or program	Contact person and phone number	Mailing address	Date I sent letter to request information.
1				
2				
3				
4				
5				

Barrier: _____

Possible solutions:

1. _____

2. _____

3. _____

List resources in your release community that offers assistance with this barrier:

	Name of agency or program	Contact person and phone number	Mailing address	Date I sent letter to request information.
1				
2				
3				
4				
5				

Finances/Budget

If you are able to have money saved for your release, you will be a step ahead of most. Walking out of prison with money in your pocket will give you a sense of accomplishment and build into your self-worth. Of course, money does not determine one's worth, but I think we can all agree that it helps us feel more secure and provides a sense of independence. You may laugh at the prospect of being able to save money in prison, since most prison jobs pay next to nothing. Please don't let this discourage you. If you set a savings goal of just 10-20 percent of all money you receive, you'll find that even small amounts add up. Some prisons have a reentry savings account program that you can put money into. This is a good option because it keeps your savings money out of your regular spending account. This is similar to having both a savings and checking account at a bank. Your savings is there if you need it for emergencies, but other than that you only spend what is in your checking account. You should look at your needs after prison as an "emergency" and save accordingly. Remember not to focus too much on the amount you're able to save, but put more energy into the habit of saving a percentage each time you receive money. If you can develop this into a faithful practice, you will have accomplished something that most people — in and out of prison — have not been able to do.

Creating a budget is also a good practice. This will allow you to recognize what you have to spend money on and what you want to spend money on. A budget will expose your spending habits and allow you to make adjustments that will better serve your goals. When making decisions about whether or not you should spend money on something, you can do your T.R.U.T.H. work to help you decide. The T.R.U.T.H. process can be used when thinking about small or large purchases. Thinking through each purchase and determining how it will serve you will help you determine if it's something you need or something you want. Recognizing a purchase as a want and not a need doesn't automatically mean you shouldn't purchase it. Only you can decide if spending money on something you want and don't necessarily need is going to serve the life you're trying to create. An important question to keep in mind might be, "Is what I'm thinking about buying more important than what I will need after I release?" It's easy to get caught up in wanting to make your time in prison more comfortable. In prison, you have lost control over a lot of aspects of your life, like when and what you eat, when you sleep, and when you can move. One thing you have some control over is how you spend your money. It feels freeing to be able to go to the store and purchase items like food, clothing, and hygiene items. The true challenge is to remain focused on the big picture: your release. Most of the items you can purchase in prison are not as important as what you will need money for after you release. Again, doing your T.R.U.T.H. work with your finances will guide you towards the life you desire.

T.R.U.T.H. work example

T — The Thing might be that there is a special day or event coming up. You and several of your friends would like to chip in and celebrate with extra food from the store. Your release date is in two months, and you've managed to save $100 to have when you get out. R — Recognize your thoughts about this situation. You really want to pitch in and get some extra food for the celebration. This might be your last time to celebrate with your friends before your release. But you know you're going to need every dime you have after you release. U — Understand your feelings that come up with each of these thoughts. Being able to contribute to and participate in the celebration makes you feel included and perhaps needed for the celebration to be a good one. On the other hand, spending the money you have saved for your release makes you feel irresponsible and nervous. T — Think about your actions in each of these scenarios. You decide to go to the store and spend $20 of your savings on extra food for the celebration. Or, you decide not to spend any of the money you've saved. H — How do each of these decisions serve you? Only you can decide that.

<u>**Chapter Notes & Key Takeaways:**</u>

BUDGET WORKSHEET

Monthly Expenses

Savings (to set aside)	$_____
Child Support	$_____
Rent/Mortgage	$_____
Utilities	$_____
Home insurance/tax	$_____
Credit Card Payment	$_____
Groceries	$_____
Eating out	$_____
Coffee/Snacks	$_____
Car Payment	$_____
Car Insurance/Tax	$_____
Car Maintenance	$_____
Gas	$_____
Public Transit/Tolls	$_____
Day Care	$_____
Allowances	$_____
Clothing	$_____
Toiletries and Care	$_____
Haircuts	$_____
Gym	$_____
Health/Life Insurance	$_____
Doctor/Dentist Visits	$_____
Prescription	$_____
Tuition	$_____
Books/Fees	$_____
Tickets-Entertainment	$_____
Cable/Dish	$_____
Internet	$_____
Netflix	$_____
Gifts	$_____
Pet Supplies	$_____
Cell Phone	$_____
Restitution/Legal Fees	$_____
Others	$_____
EXPENSES TOTAL	$_____

Monthly Income

Employment	$_____
VA Benefits	$_____
Social Security	$_____
Disability	$_____
Food Stamps	$_____
Family Assistance	$_____
INCOME TOTAL	$_____

Income Total-Expenses Total=Spendable

_____ - _____ = _____

Is this amount in the negative or positive?

Where can you cut back?

How can you make supplemental legal income?

Chapter 6

Reentry Toolbox

Social Security card, birth certificate, state ID, driver's license

There are specific documents that you will want to have when you release from prison. For example, your Social Security card and your birth certificate will be vital in getting your state photo ID when you release. Being able to obtain your state photo ID or driver's license as soon as you release will allow you to immediately apply for resources and employment. Some prisons may provide a state photo ID before you release, and if you are at one of those facilities, then you are a step ahead of the rest. Birth certificates are easy to get. Each state has its own application and charges its own processing fee. Again, some prisons pay this fee for you, and others do not. Find out if you can order a copy of your birth certificate so you can have it in hand when you release. If you think you have a copy filed away at home, ask someone to find it and confirm that it's there. If you are releasing to the same state you were born in, then it shouldn't be too time consuming to get your birth certificate after you release; just remember that this is a task you will have to do before you can get your state ID.

If you don't have a Social Security card on file, it shouldn't be difficult to get a replacement. Some prisons have a process in place to assist with getting replacement cards before release. You should check with your prison counselor or case manager to see if your facility has an established process. If they do not, you should fill out and mail the application for a replacement card before you release. Ideally, you will have your Social Security card in hand when you release.

Do you know the status of your driver's license? Is it suspended or revoked? Thinking about getting out of prison and not being able to get your license can cause anxiety and frustration. There are a couple things you can do before you get out to help ease your mind. You should first write the Department of Motor Vehicles (DMV) main office in your state. Every state has this office, and it is usually in the capital city. The letter can simply state that you are preparing for your release from prison and would like to know the status of your driver's license. It will typically take four to six weeks to get a reply. If you don't get a reply within that time frame, you can always send the letter again. Once you get a reply back from them, you should know exactly what you need to do to get your license. If you owe court fines because of traffic violations, consider writing the court and asking for them to accept time served in lieu of the fines. Not all courts will allow this, but it's worth a shot. Some courts may take a lesser payoff than the initial amount, and some may let you make payments. Something as simple as opening this communication with the courts shows that you are thinking ahead to the life you want to create.

Here is a sample letter to send the Department of Motor Vehicles in your state.

(Print name) (Number)
Address: _____
_____
_____
Date of Birth:_____
To: (address of Department of Motor Vehicles in your state)
_____
_____
_____
_____

RE: Status of Driver's License:
I am currently serving a prison sentence at _____.
                 (name of facility)

In preparation for my release, I am requesting to verify the status of my driver's license. Will you please provide me with any information you may have concerning this request, or any instructions that I may need in order to reestablish my driving privileges? Thank you.
 Sincerely,

*Enclosed: Copy of Inmate ID (if possible)

DMV Addresses

Alaska
IVR Registration
3300 B Fairbanks St.
Anchorage, AK 99503

Arizona
Arizona Motor Vehicle Division
PO Box 2100
Mail Drop 539M
Phoenix, AZ 85001

Arkansas
Arkansas Driving Records
Room 127
PO Box 1272
Little Rock, AR 72203

California
California Department of Motor Vehicles
Office of Information Services
Public Operations Unit G199
PO Box 944247
Sacramento, CA 94244

Colorado
Colorado Department of Revenue, Motor Vehicle Division
1881 Pierce St.
Lakewood, CO 80214

Connecticut
Connecticut Department of Motor Vehicles
60 State St.
Wethersfield, CT 06161

Delaware
Delaware Motor Vehicles Dept
PO Box 698
Dover, DE 19901

District of Columbia
Department of Motor Vehicles
65 K Street, NE
Washington, D.C. 20002

Florida
Bureau of Records
PO Box 5775
Tallahassee, FL 32314

Georgia
Georgia Department of Public Safety
MVR Unit
PO Box 1456
Atlanta, GA 30371

Hawaii
Hawaii Motor Vehicle and Licensing Division
1031 Nuuanu Avenue
Honolulu, HI 96817

Idaho
Idaho Transportation Department
Vehicle Services/Special Plates
PO Box 34
Boise, ID 83731

Illinois
Illinois Secretary of State
2701 S. Dirksen Parkway
Springfield, IL 62723

Indiana
Indiana Bureau of Motor Vehicles
100 N. Senate Ave.
Indianapolis, IN 46204

Iowa
Iowa Office of Driver Services
100 Euclid Ave.
PO Box 9204
Des Moines, IA 50306

Kansas
Kansas Department of Revenue
Kansas Division Of Motor Vehicles
PO Box 2188
Topeka, KS 66601

Kentucky
Kentucky Transportation Cabinet
Division of Driver Licensing
501 High Street
Frankfort, KY 40622

Louisiana
Office of Motor Vehicles
PO Box 64886
Baton Rouge, LA 70896

Maine
Bureau of Motor Vehicles
29 State House Station
Augusta, ME 04333

Maryland
Maryland Department of Transportation
Motor Vehicle Administration
6601 Ritchie Highway, N.E.
Glen Burnie, MD 21062

Massachusetts
Massachusetts Registry of Motor Vehicles
Driver Control Unit
Attn: Court Records
PO Box 199150
Boston, MA 02119

Michigan
Michigan Department of State
Record Lookup Unit
7064 Crowner Drive
Lansing, Michigan 48918

Minnesota
Minnesota Department of Public Safety
Driver and Vehicle Services
445 Minnesota Street
St. Paul, MN 55101

Mississippi
Mississippi Department of Public Safety
Driver Records Branch
PO Box 958
Jackson, MS 39205

Missouri
Drivers License Bureau
PO Box 200
Jefferson City MO 65105

Montana
Montana Records and Driver Control Bureau
Second Floor, Scott Hart Building
PO Box 201430
303 N. Roberts
Helena, MT 59620

Nebraska
Nebraska Department of Motor Vehicles
State Office Building
301 Centennial Mall South
Lincoln, NE 68509

Nevada
Nevada Department of Motor Vehicles and Public Safety
Drivers License Division
555 Wright Way
Carson City, NV 89711

New Hampshire
James H. Hayes Building
10 Hazen Drive
Concord, NH 03305

New Jersey
New Jersey Motor Vehicle Services
PO Box 160
225 East State St.
Trenton, NJ 08666

New Mexico
New Mexico Motor Vehicle Division
PO Box 1028
Joseph Montoya Bldg.
Santa Fe, NM 87504

New York
New York State Department of Motor Vehicles
6 Empire State Plaza Room 430
Albany, NY 12228

North Carolina
North Carolina DMV
Driver License Section
1100 New Bern Ave.
Raleigh, NC 27697

North Dakota
North Dakota Drivers License & Traffic Safety
608 E Boulevard Ave
Bismarck, ND 58505

Ohio
Ohio Bureau of Motor Vehicles
PO Box 16520
Columbus, OH 43266

Oklahoma
Oklahoma Department of Public Safety
3600 North Martin Luther King Blvd
Oklahoma City, OK 73111

Oregon
Oregon DMV Headquarters
Attn: Record Services
1905 Lana Ave. NE
Salem, OR, 97314

Pennsylvania
Pennsylvania Department of Transportation
Bureau of Driver Licensing
Driver Record Services
PO Box 68695
Harrisburg, PA 17106

Rhode Island
Division of Motor Vehicles
286 Main Street
Pawtucket, RI 02860

South Carolina
Division of Motor Vehicles
PO Box 1498
Columbia, SC 29216

South Dakota
South Dakota Department of Commerce and Regulation
Drivers License
118 West Capitol
Pierre, SD 57501

Tennessee
Tennessee Department of Safety
1150 Foster Avenue
Nashville, TN 37249

Texas
Texas Department of Public Safety
P O Box 4087
Austin, Texas 78773-0001

Utah
Administrative Office
210 North 1950 West
Salt Lake City, UT 84134

Vermont
Vermont Agency of Transportation
Department Of Motor Vehicles
120 State Street
Montpelier, VT 05603

Virginia
Virginia Department of Motor Vehicles
PO Box 27412
Richmond, VA 23269

Washington
Department of Licensing
PO Box 9030
Olympia, WA 98507

West Virginia
West Virginia Division of Motor Vehicles
1800 Kanawha Boulevard East
Charleston, WV 25317

Wisconsin
Wisconsin Department of Transportation
PO Box 7995
4802 Sheboygan Avenue
Madison, WI 53707

Wyoming
Wyoming Department of Transportation / Driver Services
PO Box 1708
Cheyenne, WY 82003

Birth Certificate Processing Fee by State
(at time of publication of this book)

State	Fee
Alabama	$15.00
Alaska	$30.00
Arizona	$20.00
Arkansas	$12.00
California	$25.00
Colorado	$17.75
Connecticut	$30.00
Delaware	$25.00
Florida	$9.00
Georgia	$25.00
Hawaii	$10.00
Idaho	$16.00
Illinois	$15.00
Indiana	$10.00
Iowa	$20.00
Kansas	$15.00
Kentucky	$10.00
Louisiana	$15.00
Maine	$15.00
Maryland	$10.00
Massachusetts	$32.00
Michigan	$34.00
Minnesota	$26.00
Mississippi	$17.00
Missouri	$15.00
Montana	$12.00
Nebraska	$17.00
Nevada	$20.00
New Hampshire	$15.00

New Jersey	$25.00
New Mexico	$10.00
New York	$30.00
North Carolina	$24.00
North Dakota	$7.00
Ohio	$21.50
Oklahoma	$15.00
Oregon	$25.00
Pennsylvania	$20.00
Rhode Island	$20.00
South Carolina	$12.00
South Dakota	$15.00
Tennessee	$15.00
Texas	$22.00
Utah	$20.00
Vermont	$10.00
Virginia	$12.00
Washington	$20.00
West Virginia	$12.00
Wisconsin	$20.00
Wyoming	$8.00

Form SS-5 (11-2019) UF
Discontinue Prior Editions
SOCIAL SECURITY ADMINISTRATION

OMB No. 0960-0066

Application for a Social Security Card

Applying for a Social Security Card is free!
USE THIS APPLICATION TO:

- Apply for an original Social Security card
- Apply for a replacement Social Security card
- Change or correct information on your Social Security number record

IMPORTANT: You MUST provide a properly completed application and the required evidence before we can process your application. We can only accept original documents or documents certified by the custodian of the original record. Notarized copies or photocopies which have not been certified by the custodian of the record are not acceptable. We will return any documents submitted with your application. For assistance call us at 1-800-772-1213 or visit our website at www.socialsecurity.gov.

Original Social Security Card

To apply for an original card, you must provide at least two documents to prove age, identity, and U.S. citizenship or current lawful, work-authorized immigration status. If you are not a U.S. citizen and do not have DHS work authorization, you must prove that you have a valid non-work reason for requesting a card. See page 2 for an explanation of acceptable documents.

NOTE: If you are age 12 or older and have never received a Social Security number, you must apply in person.

Replacement Social Security Card

To apply for a replacement card, you must provide one document to prove your identity. If you were born outside the U.S., you must also provide documents to prove your U.S. citizenship or current, lawful, work-authorized status. See page 2 for an explanation of acceptable documents.

Changing Information on Your Social Security Record

To change the information on your Social Security number record (i.e., a name or citizenship change, or corrected date of birth) you must provide documents to prove your identity, support the requested change, and establish the reason for the change. For example, you may provide a birth certificate to show your correct date of birth. A document supporting a name change must be recent and identify you by both your old and new names. If the name change event occurred over two years ago or if the name change document does not have enough information to prove your identity, you must also provide documents to prove your identity in your prior name and/or in some cases your new legal name. If you were born outside the U.S. you must provide a document to prove your U.S. citizenship or current lawful, work-authorized status. See page 2 for an explanation of acceptable documents.

LIMITS ON REPLACEMENT SOCIAL SECURITY CARDS

Public Law 108-458 limits the number of replacement Social Security cards you may receive to 3 per calendar year and 10 in a lifetime. Cards issued to reflect changes to your legal name or changes to a work authorization legend do not count toward these limits. We may also grant exceptions to these limits if you provide evidence from an official source to establish that a Social Security card is required.

IF YOU HAVE ANY QUESTIONS

If you have any questions about this form or about the evidence documents you must provide, please visit our website at www.socialsecurity.gov for additional information as well as locations of our offices and Social Security Card Centers. You may also call Social Security at 1-800-772-1213. You can also find your nearest office or Card Center in your local phone book.

Form SS-5 (11-2019) UF

EVIDENCE DOCUMENTS

The following lists are examples of the types of documents you must provide with your application and are not all inclusive. Call us at 1-800-772-1213 if you cannot provide these documents.

IMPORTANT : If you are completing this application on behalf of someone else, you must provide evidence that shows your authority to sign the application as well as documents to prove your identity and the identity of the person for whom you are filing the application. We can only accept original documents or documents certified by the custodian of the original record. Notarized copies or photocopies which have not been certified by the custodian of the record are not acceptable.

Evidence of Age

In general, you must provide your birth certificate. In some situations, we may accept another document that shows your age. Some of the other documents we may accept are:

- U.S. hospital record of your birth (created at the time of birth)
- Religious record established before age five showing your age or date of birth
- Passport
- Final Adoption Decree (the adoption decree must show that the birth information was taken from the original birth certificate)

Evidence of Identity

You must provide current, unexpired evidence of identity in your legal name. Your legal name will be shown on the Social Security card. Generally, we prefer to see documents issued in the U.S. Documents you submit to establish identity must show your legal name AND provide biographical information (your date of birth, age, or parents' names) **and/or** physical information (photograph, or physical description - height, eye and hair color, etc.). If you send a photo identity document but do not appear in person, the document must show your biographical information (e.g., your date of birth, age, or parents' names). Generally, documents without an expiration date should have been issued within the past two years for adults and within the past four years for children.

As proof of your identity, you must provide a:

- U.S. driver's license; or
- U.S. State-issued non-driver identity card; or
- U.S. passport

If you do not have one of the documents above or cannot get a replacement within 10 work days, we may accept other documents that show your legal name and biographical information, such as a U.S. military identity card, Certificate of Naturalization, employee identity card, certified copy of medical record (clinic, doctor or hospital), health insurance card, Medicaid card, or school identity card/record. For young children, we may accept medical records (clinic, doctor, or hospital) maintained by the medical provider. We may also accept a final adoption decree, or a school identity card, or other school record maintained by the school.

If you are not a U.S. citizen, we must see your current U.S. immigration document(s) and your foreign passport with biographical information or photograph.

WE CANNOT ACCEPT A BIRTH CERTIFICATE, HOSPITAL SOUVENIR BIRTH CERTIFICATE, SOCIAL SECURITY CARD STUB OR A SOCIAL SECURITY RECORD as evidence of identity.

Evidence of U.S. Citizenship

In general, you must provide your U.S. birth certificate or U.S. Passport. Other documents you may provide are a Consular Report of Birth, Certificate of Citizenship, or Certificate of Naturalization.

Evidence of Immigration Status

You must provide a current unexpired document issued to you by the Department of Homeland Security (DHS) showing your immigration status, such as Form I-551, I-94, or I-766. If you are an international student or exchange visitor, you may need to provide additional documents, such as Form I-20, DS-2019, or a letter authorizing employment from your school and employer (F-1) or sponsor (J-1). We CANNOT accept a receipt showing you applied for the document. If you are not authorized to work in the U.S., we can issue you a Social Security card only if you need the number for a valid non-work reason. Your card will be marked to show you cannot work and if you do work, we will notify DHS. See page 3, item 5 for more information.

Form **SS-5** (11-2019) UF

HOW TO COMPLETE THIS APPLICATION

Complete and sign this application LEGIBLY using ONLY black or blue ink on the attached or downloaded form using only 8 ½" x 11" (or A4 8.25" x 11.7") paper.

GENERAL: Items on the form are self-explanatory or are discussed below. The numbers match the numbered items on the form. If you are completing this form for someone else, please complete the items as they apply to that person.

4. Show the month, day, and full (4 digit) year of birth; for example, "1998" for year of birth.

5. If you check "Legal Alien Not Allowed to Work" or "Other," you must provide a document from a U.S. Federal, State, or local government agency that explains why you need a Social Security number and that you meet all the requirements for the government benefit. NOTE: Most agencies do not require that you have a Social Security number. Contact us to see if your reason qualifies for a Social Security number.

6., 7. Providing race and ethnicity information is voluntary and is requested for informational and statistical purposes only. Your choice whether to answer or not does not affect decisions we make on your application. If you do provide this information, we will treat it very carefully.

9.B., 10.B. If you are applying for an original Social Security card for a child under age 18, you MUST show the parents' Social Security numbers unless the parent was never assigned a Social Security number. If the number is not known and you cannot obtain it, check the "unknown" box.

13. If the date of birth you show in item 4 is different from the date of birth currently shown on your Social Security record, show the date of birth currently shown on your record in item 13 and provide evidence to support the date of birth shown in item 4.

16. Show an address where you can receive your card 7 to 14 days from now.

17. WHO CAN SIGN THE APPLICATION? If you are age 18 or older and are physically and mentally capable of reading and completing the application, you must sign in item 17. If you are under age 18, you may either sign yourself, or a parent or legal guardian may sign for you. If you are over age 18 and cannot sign on your own behalf, a legal guardian, parent, or close relative may generally sign for you. If you cannot sign your name, you should sign with an "X" mark and have two people sign as witnesses in the space beside the mark. Please do not alter your signature by including additional information on the signature line as this may invalidate your application. Call us if you have questions about who may sign your application.

HOW TO SUBMIT THIS APPLICATION

In most cases, you can take or mail this signed application with your documents to any Social Security office. Any documents you mail to us will be returned to you. Go to https://secure.ssa.gov/apps6z/FOLO/fo001.jsp to find the Social Security office or Social Security Card Center that serves your area.

Form SS-5 (11-2019) UF   Page 4 of 5

PROTECT YOUR SOCIAL SECURITY NUMBER AND CARD

Protect your SSN card and number from loss and identity theft. DO NOT carry your SSN card with you. Keep it in a secure location and only take it with you when you must show the card; e.g., to obtain a new job, open a new bank account, or to obtain benefits from certain U.S. agencies. Use caution in giving out your Social Security number to others, particularly during phone, mail, email and Internet requests you did not initiate.

PRIVACY ACT STATEMENT
Collection and Use of Personal Information

Sections 205(c) and 702 of the Social Security Act, as amended, allow us to collect this information. Furnishing us this information is voluntary. However, failing to provide all or part of the information may prevent us from assigning you a Social Security number (SSN) and issuing you a new or replacement Social Security card.

We will use the information to assign you an SSN and issue you a new or replacement Social Security card. We may also share your information for the following purposes, called routine uses:

- To Federal, State, and local entities to assist them with administering income maintenance and health maintenance programs, when a Federal statute authorizes them to use the SSN; and,

- To the Department of State for administering the Social Security Act in foreign countries through its facilities and services.

In addition, we may share this information in accordance with the Privacy Act and other Federal laws. For example, where authorized, we may use and disclose this information in computer matching programs, in which our records are compared with other records to establish or verify a person's eligibility for Federal benefit programs and for repayment of incorrect or delinquent debts under these programs.

A list of additional routine uses is available in our Privacy Act System of Records Notice (SORN) 60-0058, entitled Master Files of Social Security Number (SSN) Holders and SSN Applications, as published in the Federal Register (FR) on December 29, 2010, at 75 FR 82121. Additional information, and a full listing of all of our SORNs, is available on our website at www.ssa.gov/privacy.

Paperwork Reduction Act Statement - This information collection meets the requirements of 44 U.S.C. § 3507, as amended by section 2 of the Paperwork Reduction Act of 1995. You do not need to answer these questions unless we display a valid Office of Management and Budget control number. We estimate that it will take about 8.5 to 9.5 minutes to read the instructions, gather the facts, and answer the questions. **SEND OR BRING THE COMPLETED FORM TO YOUR LOCAL SOCIAL SECURITY OFFICE. You can find your local Social Security office through SSA's website at www.socialsecurity.gov. Offices are also listed under U. S. Government agencies in your telephone directory or you may call Social Security at 1-800-772-1213 (TTY 1-800-325-0778).** *You may send comments on our time estimate above to: SSA, 6401 Security Blvd, Baltimore, MD 21235-6401.* **Send only** *comments relating to our time estimate to this address, not the completed form.*

Form SS-5 (11-2019) UF
Discontinue Prior Editions
SOCIAL SECURITY ADMINISTRATION

OMB No. 0960-0066

Application for a Social Security Card

1
- NAME TO BE SHOWN ON CARD: First / Full Middle Name / Last
- FULL NAME AT BIRTH IF OTHER THAN ABOVE: First / Full Middle Name / Last
- OTHER NAMES USED

2 Social Security number previously assigned to the person listed in item 1

3 PLACE OF BIRTH (Do Not Abbreviate) City / State or Foreign Country / Office Use Only FCI

4 DATE OF BIRTH MM/DD/YYYY

5 CITIZENSHIP (Check One)
- ☐ U.S. Citizen
- ☐ Legal Alien Allowed To Work
- ☐ Legal Alien Not Allowed To Work (See Instructions On Page 3)
- ☐ Other (See Instructions On Page 3)

6 ETHNICITY — Are You Hispanic or Latino? (Your Response is Voluntary)
- ☐ Yes ☐ No

7 RACE — Select One or More (Your Response is Voluntary)
- ☐ Native Hawaiian
- ☐ Alaska Native
- ☐ Asian
- ☐ American Indian
- ☐ Black/African American
- ☐ Other Pacific Islander
- ☐ White

8 SEX: ☐ Male ☐ Female

9
- A. PARENT/MOTHER'S NAME AT HER BIRTH: First / Full Middle Name / Last
- B. PARENT/MOTHER'S SOCIAL SECURITY NUMBER (See instructions for 9B on Page 3) ☐ Unknown

10
- A. PARENT/FATHER'S NAME: First / Full Middle Name / Last
- B. PARENT/FATHER'S SOCIAL SECURITY NUMBER (See instructions for 10B on Page 3) ☐ Unknown

11 Has the person listed in item 1 or anyone acting on his/her behalf ever filed for or received a Social Security number card before?
- ☐ Yes (If "yes" answer questions 12-13)
- ☐ No
- ☐ Don't Know (If "don't know," skip to question 14.)

12 Name shown on the most recent Social Security card issued for the person listed in item 1: First / Full Middle Name / Last

13 Enter any different date of birth if used on an earlier application for a card: MM/DD/YYYY

14 TODAY'S DATE MM/DD/YYYY

15 DAYTIME PHONE NUMBER: Area Code / Number

16 MAILING ADDRESS (Do Not Abbreviate): Street Address, Apt. No., PO Box, Rural Route No. / City / State/Foreign Country / ZIP Code

I declare under penalty of perjury that I have examined all the information on this form, and on any accompanying statements or forms, and it is true and correct to the best of my knowledge.

17 YOUR SIGNATURE

18 YOUR RELATIONSHIP TO THE PERSON IN ITEM 1 IS:
- ☐ Self
- ☐ Natural Or Adoptive Parent
- ☐ Legal Guardian
- ☐ Other Specify ____

DO NOT WRITE BELOW THIS LINE (FOR SSA USE ONLY)

NPN			DOC	NTI	CAN		ITV
PBC	EVI	EVA	EVC	PRA	NWR	DNR	UNIT

EVIDENCE SUBMITTED

SIGNATURE AND TITLE OF EMPLOYEE(S) REVIEWING EVIDENCE AND/OR CONDUCTING INTERVIEW

DATE

DCL / DATE

Credit

Do you know what your credit score is? Do you know what is on your credit report? Maybe you'll worry about that later when it becomes an issue. However, knowing what is on your credit report will allow you to begin repairing or building your credit now — before it becomes an issue. Credit scores are used to determine eligibility by many agencies, not necessarily just when applying for a loan. Everyone is allowed one free credit report per year from all three credit agencies: TransUnion, Equifax, and Experian.

It is not uncommon for people in prison to get their credit report and find accounts listed that have been opened while they were incarcerated. If you get your credit report and believe there is incorrect information on it, you can dispute the accounts and potentially have them removed. For instance, if there is an account on your credit report that has been opened since you've been in prison, you simply send them a letter or document that shows your dates of incarceration. The credit agencies will have to remove that account from your report. If there are delinquent accounts on your report that are over seven years old, you can list these accounts in a letter and ask for them to be removed from your report. Another option to help repair poor credit history is to contact the creditors and ask for a settlement amount. Many are willing to accept a payment much lower than you owe in order to settle the account and close it out.

Taking the necessary steps now to repair your credit will serve you greatly after you release. The first step is filling out and mailing in the Annual Credit Report Request form. You should include a supplemental letter with your identifying information and request. You may also want to include a letter of incarceration. This letter has to be written by a staff member at your facility. Typically, a counselor or case manager will prepare this letter, but this may not be the case at your facility. Sending these letters with the application will further prove your identity and verify your address at the prison.

Annual Credit Report Request Form

EQUIFAX **experian** **TransUnion**

You have the right to get a free copy of your credit file disclosure, commonly called a credit report, once every 12 months, from each of the nationwide consumer credit reporting companies - Equifax, Experian and TransUnion.

For instant access to your free credit report, visit www.annualcreditreport.com.

For more information on obtaining your free credit report, visit www.annualcreditreport.com or call 877-322-8228.

Use this form if you prefer to write to request your credit report from any, or all, of the nationwide consumer credit reporting companies. The following information is required to process your request. **Omission of any information may delay your request.**

Once complete, fold (do not staple or tape), place into a #10 envelope, affix required postage and mail to:
Annual Credit Report Request Service P.O. Box 105281 Atlanta, GA 30348-5281.

Please use a Black or Blue Pen and write your responses in PRINTED CAPITAL LETTERS without touching the sides of the boxes like the examples listed below:

`A B C D E F G H I J K L M N O P Q R S T U V W X Y Z   0 1 2 3 4 5 6 7 8 9`

Social Security Number: [ ][ ][ ] - [ ][ ] - [ ][ ][ ][ ]

Date of Birth: [ ][ ] / [ ][ ] / [ ][ ][ ][ ]
Month / Day / Year

— Fold Here — — Fold Here —

First Name: [...]   **M.I.:** [ ]
Last Name: [...]   **JR, SR, III, etc.:** [ ]

Current Mailing Address:
House Number [...] Street Name [...]
Apartment Number / Private Mailbox [...]   For Puerto Rico Only: Print Urbanization Name [...]
City [...]   State [ ]   ZipCode [ ]

Previous Mailing Address (complete only if at current mailing address for less than two years):
House Number [...] Street Name [...]

— Fold Here — — Fold Here —

Apartment Number / Private Mailbox [...]   For Puerto Rico Only: Print Urbanization Name [...]
City [...]   State [ ]   ZipCode [ ]

Shade Circle Like This → ●
Not Like This → ⊗ ⊘

I want a credit report from (shade each that you would like to receive):
○ Equifax
○ Experian
○ TransUnion

○ Shade here if, for security reasons, you want your credit report to include no more than the last four digits of your Social Security Number.

If additional information is needed to process your request, the consumer credit reporting company will contact you by mail.

Your request will be processed within 15 days of receipt and then mailed to you.

Copyright 2004, Central Source LLC

31238

G-1

Date:_____

Annual Credit Report Request Service
P.O. Box 105281
Atlanta GA 30348-5281

I am currently incarcerated in prison at_____.
                                                (name of facility)

I would like to request a copy of my credit reports.

_____
(Name & number)
Address: _____
_____
_____

Full Legal Name: _____
DOB: _____
Social Security Number: _____

Thank You,

*enclosed: copy of prison identification card (if possible)

Letter of Incarceration should be typed by staff on the facility's letterhead.

                                          Date:

Name:
Prison Register Number:

RE: Letter of Incarceration/ Proof of Address

To Whom it May Concern,

_____ is an inmate at _____. He/She has been in custody since _____ and is scheduled to release on _____.

Current mailing address is:
Name & Number:_____

Address: _____

            _____

            _____

Thank You,

Name/Title

Child Support

Current statistics show that one in every twenty-eight kids in America has a parent in prison. That is why taking care of child support issues is so important. It is not uncommon for a parent to release from prison owing thousands of dollars in back child support. Child support agencies used to consider incarceration as "voluntary unemployment." This is no longer the case in most, if not all, states. States will modify a child support order while you are in prison based on the significant change in your income. The modification is not done automatically. It is up to you to contact them and let them know you are in prison. You can fill out a modification request form and mail it to the child support office where your order was issued. If you don't have this address, you can mail your modification request to the main child support office in your state. Typically, this office will forward your request to the local office. If you are transferred to another prison, it is up to you to notify the child support office of your new address. Failing to do this could result in you missing important notifications.

It is possible to have a child support order and not know it. If the person who has custody of your child is on any type of public assistance, then the state will issue an order for child support to be paid by the non-custodial parent. This order will accumulate each month whether you know about it or not. So, if you have a minor child, it is worth your time to verify whether you have an order and then take the necessary action to modify the order while you're in prison. Once you release, it is your responsibility to notify your local child support office. Having open communication with the child support office and being honest about your situation will allow them to put a plan in place that works for you.

REQUEST FOR AGENCY REVIEW OF CHILD SUPPORT

Mail your request to: (child support office address)

Dear Sir/Madam:

- I am currently incarcerated at _____. My incarceration resulted in a substantial decrease in my earnings, which makes my existing child support order unreasonable and unfair. I respectfully request that the child support agency review my case. If the review shows that my case meets the criteria for modification, I request that the county initiate a modification action.
- Currently, I have income from the following sources: _____
- I was admitted into custody on:_____
- I was previously incarcerated in prison or county jail on the following dates: _____
- My anticipated release date is:_____
- I am financially unable to pay support due to incarceration of at least 30 days for an offense other than the nonpayment of child support and therefore request the court order interest to stop accruing on the child support debt or arrearages.
- I request the county child support office review any arrearages that have accrued on my case for possible adjustment.

Personal Information:

First Name:	Middle Name:	Last Name:
SS #:	Birth Date:	Offender ID#:
Date:	Signature:	

IMPORTANT NOTICE

Submitting this request does not guarantee your child support order with be modified. Your request will be reviewed and a reply sent to you at:

Name & Reg Number:_____

Your Address: _____

_____

_____

ALL CHILD SUPPORT ENFORCEMENT AGENCIES

State	Address	Phone Number(s)	
Alabama	Department of Human Resources 50 Ripley Street P.O. Box 304000 Montgomery, Alabama 36130 - 1801	**Office:**	(334) 242-1425 (P) (334)24-0606 (F)
Alaska	Child Support Services Division Department of Revenue 550 West 7th Avenue, Suite 280 Anchorage, Alaska 99501-6699	**Office:**	1- (800) 478-3300 (P) (907) 787-3220 (F)
Arizona	Division of Child Support Enforcement, Arizona Department of Economic Security 3443 N. Central, 4th Floor Phoenix, Arizona 85012	**Office:**	602-252-4045(P) 602-771-8191(F)
Arkansas	Office of Child Support Enforcement, Department of Finance and Administration PO Box 8133 Little Rock, Arkansas 72203-8133	**Office:**	501-682-8398(P) 501-682-6002(F)
California	California Dept. of Child Support Services P.O. Box 419064 , Mail Station - 10 Rancho Cordova, California 95741-9064	**Office:**	916-464-5300(P) 916-464-5211(F)
Colorado	Division of Child Support Enforcement, Department of Human Services 1575 Sherman St., 5th floor Denver, Colorado 80203-1714	**Office:**	303-866-4300(P) 303-866-4360(F)
Connecticut	Connecticut Department of Social Services, Bureau of Child Support Enforcement 25 Sigourney Street Hartford, Connecticut 06106	**Office:**	860-424-4989(P) 860-951-2996(F)
Delaware	Division of Child Support Enforcement, Delaware Health and Social Services P.O. Box 11223 Wilmington, Delaware 19850	**Office:** **Cust. Svc.:**	302-395-6500(P) 302-395-6733(F) 302-577-7171
District of Columbia	Child Support Services Division, Office of the Attorney General Judiciary Square 441 Fourth Street NW 5th Floor Washington, District of Columbia 20001	**Office:** **Cust. Svc.:**	202-724-2131(P) 202-724-3710(F) 202-442-9900
Florida	Child Support Enforcement, Department of Revenue P.O. Box 8030 Tallahassee, Florida 32399-7016	**Office:** **Cust. Svc. :**	850-717-7000(P) 850-921-0792(F) 1-800-622-5437
Georgia	Child Support Services, Department of Human Resources 2 Peachtree Street, Room 20-460 Atlanta, Georgia 30303	**Office:**	404-657-3851(P) 404-657-3326(F)
Guam	Office of the Attorney General, Child Support Enforcement Division 287 West O'Brien Drive Hagatna, Guam 96910	**Office:**	671-475-3360(P) 671-475-3203(F)
Hawaii	Child Support Enforcement Agency, Department of the Attorney General 601 Kamokila Boulevard, Suite 207 Kapolei, Hawaii 96707	**Office:**	808-692-7000(P) 808-692-7134(F)

State	Address		Phone
Idaho	Bureau of Child Support Services Department of Health and Welfare P.O. Box 83720 Boise, Idaho 83720-0036	**Office:**	800-356-9868(P) 208-334-5571(F)
Illinois	Division of Child Support Enforcement, Illinois Department of Healthcare and Family Services 509 S. 6th St., 6th Floor Springfield, Illinois 62701	**Office:**	800-447-4278(P) 217-524-6049(F)
Indiana	Child Support Bureau, Department of Child Services 402 West Washington Street Room W360 Indianapolis, Indiana 46204-2739	**Office:**	317-233-5437(P) 317-233-4932(F)
Iowa	Bureau of Collections, Department of Human Services 400 S.W. 8th Street, Suite H Des Moines, Iowa 50319-4691	**Office:**	515-281-5647(P) 515-281-8854(F)
Kansas	Kansas Child Support Services, Department for Children and Families P.O. Box 497 Topeka, Kansas 66601-0497	**Office:**	785-296-3237(P) 785-296-8395(F)
Kentucky	Child Support Enforcement Program, Department for Income Support, Cabinet for Families and Children 730 Schenkel Lane - PO Box 2150 Frankfort, Kentucky 40602-2150	**Office:**	502-564-2285(P) 502-564-5988(F)
Louisiana	Office of Family Support, Support Enforcement Services Division P.O. Box 94065, 627 N. Fourth Street Baton Rouge, Louisiana 70802	**Office:**	225-342-4780(P) 225-342-7397(F)
Maine	Division of Support Enforcement & Recovery 11 State House Station, 19 Union Street Augusta, Maine 04333	**Office:**	207-624-4100(P) 207-287-2334(F)
Maryland	Maryland Child Support Enforcement Administration, Department of Human Resources Saratoga State Center, 311 West Saratoga Street, Room 301 Baltimore, Maryland 21201-3521	**Office:** **Customer Service:**	410-767-7065(P) 410-333-6264(F) 800-332-6347
Massachusetts	Child Support Enforcement Division, Massachusetts Department of Revenue PO Box 9561 Boston, Massachusetts 02114-9561	**Office:**	800-332-2733(P) 617-887-7570(F)
Michigan	Office of Child Support, Department of Human Services 235 South Grand Avenue, P.O. Box 30478 Lansing, Michigan 48909-7978	**Office:**	517-241-7460(P) 517-373-4980(F)
Minnesota	Office of Child Support Enforcement, Department of Human Services 444 Lafayette Road, P.O. Box #64946 St. Paul, Minnesota 55164-0946	**Office:**	651-431-4340(P) 651-431-7517(F)
Mississippi	Division of Child Support Enforcement, Department of Human Services 750 North State Street Jackson, Mississippi 39202	**Office:**	601-359-4861(P) 601-359-4415(F)
Missouri	Family Support Division P.O. Box 6790 Jefferson City, Missouri 65102-6790	**Office:**	573-751-4247(P) 573-751-0507(F)

State	Address		Phone
Montana	Child Support, Department of Public Health & Human Services 3075 N. Montana Ave. Suite 112 Helena, Montana 59620	Office:	406-444-9855(P) 406-444-1370(F)
Nebraska	Department of Health and Human Services PO Box 94728, 220 South 17th Street Lincoln, Nebraska 68509-4728	Office:	402-471-1400(P) 402-471-7311(F)
Nevada	State of Nevada Division of Welfare and Supportive Services 1470 College Parkway Carson City, Nevada 89706-7924	Office: Cust. Svc.: Cust. Svc.: Toll Free#:	775-684-0705(P) 775-684-0702(F) 775-684-7200 702-486-1646 800-992-0900
New Hampshire	Division of Child Support Services, Health & Human Services 129 Pleasant Street Concord, New Hampshire 03301-8711	Office:	800-852-3345(P) 603-271-4787(F)
New Jersey	Office of Child Support, Department of Human Services P.O. Box 716 Trenton, New Jersey 08625-0716	Office:	609-584-5093(P) 609-588-2354(F)
New Mexico	Child Support Enforcement Division, Department of Human Services P.O. Box 25110 Santa Fe, New Mexico 87502	Office:	505-476-7207(P) 505-476-7045(F)
New York	New York State, Division of Child Support Enforcement 40 North Pearl Street, 13th Floor Albany, New York 12243-0001	Office:	518-474-1078(P) 518-486-3127(F)
North Carolina	North Carolina Department of Health and Human Services, Division of Social Services, Office of Child Support Enforcement Post Office Box 20800 Raleigh, North Carolina 27619-0800	Office:	919-855-4755(P) 919-715-8174(F)
North Dakota	Child Support Enforcement Program, North Dakota Department of Human Services P.O. Box 7190 Bismarck, North Dakota 58507-7190	Office:	701-328-3582(P) 701-328-5497(F)
Ohio	Office of Child Support Enforcement, Department of Human Services and Job and Family Services 30 East Broad Street, 31st Floor Columbus, Ohio 43215-3414	Office:	614-752-6561(P) 614-752-9760(F)
Oklahoma	Oklahoma Child Support Services, Oklahoma Department of Human Services P.O. Box 53552 Oklahoma City, Oklahoma 73152	Office:	405-522-2874(P) 405-522-2753(F)
Oregon	Division of Child Support , Oregon Department of Justice 494 State Street, S.E. Suite 300 Salem, Oregon 97301	Office:	503-986-6166(P) 503-986-6158(F)
Pennsylvania	Bureau of Child Support Enforcement, Department of Public Welfare P.O. Box 8018 Harrisburg, Pennsylvania 17105-8018	Office:	800-932-0211(P) 717-787-9706(F)
Puerto Rico	Administration for Child Support Enforcement P.O. Box 70376 San Juan, Puerto Rico 00936-8376	Office:	787-767-1500 (P) 787-282-8324(F)

State	Address		Contact
Rhode Island	Office of Child Support Services, Department of Human Services 77 Dorrance Street Providence, Rhode Island 02904	**Office:**	401-458-4400(P) 401-458-4407(F)
South Carolina	Child Support Enforcement Division, Department of Social Services P.O. Box 1469 Columbia, South Carolina 29202-1469	**Office:** **toll free:**	803-898-9210(P) 803-898-9201(F) 1-800-768-5858
South Dakota	Division of Child Support, Department of Social Services 700 Governor's Drive Pierre, South Dakota 57501-2291	**Office:**	605-773-3641(P) 605-773-7295(F)
Tennessee	Child Support Division, TN Department of Human Services 15th Floor, Citizens Plaza Building, 400 Deaderick Street Nashville, Tennessee 37243-1403	**Office:**	615-313-4880(P) 615-532-2791(F)
Texas	Child Support Division, Office of the Attorney General P.O. Box 12017 Austin, Texas 78711-2017	**Office:**	800-252-8014(P) 512-460-6867(F)
Utah	Child Support Services, Department of Human Services, Office of Recovery Services P.O. Box 45033 Salt Lake, Utah 84145-0033	**Office:**	801-536-8901(P) 801-536-8509(F)
Vermont	Office of Child Support 103 South Main Street Waterbury, Vermont 05671-1901	**Office:**	802-786-3214(P) 802-241-2319(F)
Virgin Islands	U.S. Virgin Islands Department of Justice, Paternity and Child Support Division 8000 Nisky Center, 2nd Floor, Suite 500 St. Thomas, Virgin Islands 00802	**Office:** **fax/St.Croix:**	340-778-5958(P) 340-775-3808(F) 340-779-3800
Virginia	Division of Child Support Enforcement 7 N. Eighth St., 1st Floor Richmond, Virginia 23219	**Office:**	800-468-8894(P) 804-726-7476(F)
Washington	Division of Child Support Department of Social & Health Services P.O. Box 9162 Olympia, Washington 98507-9162	**Office:**	360-664-5000(P) 360-664-5444(F)
West Virginia	WV Department of Health and Human Resources, Bureau for Child Support Enforcement 350 Capitol Street, Room 147 Charleston, West Virginia 25301-3703	**Office:**	800-249-3778(P) 304-558-2445(F)
Wisconsin	Bureau of Child Support, Division of Economic Support 201 E. Washington Ave. E200 P.O. Box 7935 Madison, Wisconsin 53707-7935	**Office:**	608-266-9909(P) 608-267-2824(F)
Wyoming	Department of Family Services, Child Support Enforcement 122 W. 25th Herschler Building, 1301 1st Floor East Cheyenne, Wyoming 82002	**Office:**	307-777-6948(P) 307-777-5588(F)

Pending Legal Issues

Wouldn't it be nice if you could release from prison with an automatic "clean slate"? Unfortunately, if you had any pending legal issues before you went to prison, they will be waiting for you when you release unless you address them beforehand. Whether it is a simple traffic ticket or a charge for another crime you committed in a different jurisdiction, it's worth the effort on your part to try and resolve the issue before you release.

Find out what department at the prison can run a warrant check, and ask them to run one on you. It's a good idea to do this even if you don't think you have anything pending. Doing this earlier rather than close to your release will give you more time to attempt to resolve the issue(s). If your warrant check shows you have something pending, simply write the court a letter that states your current situation, and ask if there is a way to resolve the matter prior to your release from prison.

Depending on what the ticket or charge is, many courts are willing to work with incarcerated individuals to close these cases. It's a good idea to include a letter of incarceration with your letter to the court. This will provide verification that you are currently in prison. If you choose to write the court a letter and attempt to resolve pending legal matters, a sample letter is provided on the next page. The sample letter options are only examples of what some people have used, and they may not be what you want to use to resolve your pending legal matter. So, simply follow the format and write your specific request.

(This letter is from you)

Date:

Court Address:

_____

_____

_____

Name & Prison ID #:_____

Address: _____

_____

_____

Date of Birth:_____

Case Number &/or Charge: _____

Dear Court,
I am currently serving a _____ month/year prison sentence at _____.

Example: I am aware I have a pending violation in your court. My reason for this letter is to request to resolve this matter prior to my release from prison. I would like to respectfully ask the court to consider dismissing the above charge. I am asking the court to consider this request so I can begin preparing for my successful reentry back into society, hopefully with a clean slate. Please send return correspondence to the above address with my name and registration number listed first. Your help is greatly appreciated.

Example: I am aware that I owe outstanding fines to your court. My reason for this letter is to request to resolve this matter prior to my release from prison. I would like to respectfully ask the court to grant time served in lieu of the fines. I am begging the Court to consider this request so I can begin preparing for my successful reentry back into society. Please send return correspondence to the above address with my name and registration number listed first. Your help is greatly appreciated.

Thank you for your time and attention.

Sincerely,

Letter of Incarceration to the court should be done by a staff member on facility letterhead.

Date:

Inmate Name:_____

Prison Registration No.: _____

To _____ Court:

The above named person is an inmate currently confined at _____ serving a _____ month/year sentence. _____ has been in custody since _____ and has a projected release date of _____.

Review of his/her record indicates possible outstanding charges/tickets/warrant in your jurisdiction. We placed on him/her the burden of clarifying this information prior to referral for community placement, custody reduction, or participation in certain programs. This letter was provided to assist him/her with resolving these pending legal issues. _____ was instructed he/she may send this letter to the Court or prosecutor of the jurisdiction where charges may be pending. This letter should be accompanied by a letter from the inmate with available identifying information. Return correspondence would be appreciated, preferably on your letterhead, or marked with a stamp certifying your position with the Court.

Sincerely,

Name/Title

Chapter Notes & Key Takeaways

Chapter 7

Employment

What are you going to do to earn money when you get out of prison? Everyone needs a source of income. If you haven't already been thinking about the answer to this question, now is the time to start. Don't get hung up on the myth that just because you're a felon you will never get a good job. That is simply not true. There are certain jobs that, depending on your crime, you might not be able to get, but this is a small percentage compared to the jobs you can get. For example, if you robbed a bank, it is unlikely that a bank will hire you. If you have a drug conviction, you might not be a good candidate to work in a pharmacy. But, outside of those jobs specifically related to your crime, the possibilities are endless.

Having a job while you're in prison will help you when you release from prison and start your job search. It is important to have an employment history for the time you were incarcerated. Employers are more willing to hire felons today than ever before, but they want to see that you were productive while you were incarcerated. If you have reasons you can't work while you're in prison, you will need to be able to explain this at an interview. If you're not working, then how are you spending your time? Are you taking educational or skill-training programs? Are you involved in productive activities that are taking place in the prison? Being able to talk about these questions at a job interview will let the employer know that you spent your time in prison bettering yourself. Employers are willing to take a chance on a good candidate with a criminal background. They are more hesitant to hire those who choose to do nothing productive while in prison.

If possible, prepare your resume before you release. If you don't have access to the resources you need to create your own resume, make sure you have something that shows the jobs you worked during incarceration and the dates you worked each one. This will make it easier to prepare your resume after you release. Most communities have a public library with access to a computer. This is an option if you need to type your resume after you release and don't have a computer at home. Professionals who assist with resume writing recommend the *functional resume* for individuals with a criminal background. The functional resume allows you to list your accomplishments, employment history and education in a way that focuses on your skills and abilities. Again, make sure you list your prison jobs on your resume.

118 Sherman Drive, Prosperous, MO 39180•jimdandy@gmail.com

Jim Dandy

Objective

I want to succeed in a stimulating and challenging environment, building the success of the company while I experience advancement opportunities.

Professional Accomplishments

Welding
- Completed 240 hours of Welding Training
- Studied Blueprints & Specifications, Calculated Dimensions, Inspected Materials to be Welded, Ignited Torches, Hands-On Welding, Maintained Equipment & Machinery

Cabinetry
- Completed 240 hours of Cabinetry
- Hands-On Building, Calculating Measurements, Measuring & Cutting, Assembly & Finishing

Restaurant Management
- Serve Safe Certification
- Topics Studied: Customer Service, Budgeting, Staff Schedules, Planning Menus, Marketing & Advertising, Ordering & Storing Supplies, and Recruiting, Training & Supervising Staff

Employment History

NECC Lincoln, NE	06/2015- 10/2016	Detail Technician: Maintain High Level of Sanitation, Buff & Wax Floors, Detail all Equipment
NESW, Omaha, NE	05/2014- 06/2015	Detail Technician: Buff & Wax Floors, Sanitation, Clean & Detail all Equipment
Cleaners Detail Shop, Port Gibson, MS	03/2010- 06/2010	Team Leader, Maintain Safe Work Environment, Responsible for Daily Operations
Warehouse Sports Bar, Vicksburg, MS	07/2008- 02/2009	Maintenance Technician, Overseer of Property

Education

2014	Cabinetry Certification	Holmes Community College, Goodman, MS
2013	Welding Certification	Holmes Community College, Goodman, MS
2013	Restaurant Management	Holmes Community College, Goodman, MS
1998	GED/Carpentry	Job Corp., Gulfport, MS

References

References are available on request.

(address, email, phone)

(name)

Objective
Why do you want to work for this company? What's in it for you & what's in it for them?

Professional Accomplishments

I know how to:	*I learned how to do this by:*	
1._____	1._____	2._____
2._____	1._____	2._____
3._____	1._____	2._____

Employment History

Name of Company_____ Dates of Employment_____
Job Title/Duties_____

Name of Company_____ Dates of Employment_____
Job Title/Duties_____

Name of Company_____ Dates of Employment_____
Job Title/Duties_____

Name of Company_____ Dates of Employment_____
Job Title/Duties_____

Name of Company_____ Dates of Employment_____
Job Title/Duties_____

Education
Name of High School_____Year Graduated_____
GED- Year Earned_____
College/ Trade/Vocational:

References
References available upon request.

There are several community resources that can assist you while you are job seeking. If you have any type of disability, Vocational Rehabilitation is a nationwide organization that will assist you with finding a job. They have offices all over the United States. MERS/Goodwill is another agency that offers employment assistance (MERS is the Metropolitan Employment Rehabilitation Service, established in 1940). You will need to find out if they have an office in your community. Many communities also have nonprofits that offer employment assistance. Since each community has different resources, it will be important for you to find out what specific agencies are in your community.

Another great resource to help with employment needs is your local One Stop. In some areas they might be called a Career Center or Job Center. Almost every city has one. These centers offer employability resources such as resume writing, interview skills, computer skills, online job searches, and assistance with filling out applications. These centers typically have staff who work specifically with people with a criminal background. Employers often build relationships with these centers and reach out to them when they are hiring. Your local job center will have hiring events and job fairs and invite multiple employers who are hiring to attend. These events are a great opportunity for you to speak to many employers at one time. Registering with the job center in your area after you release should be high on your priority list.

You should know what employment agencies are in your community. If you have someone who can look them up and send you their contact information, you can write them a letter before you release and ask what services they provide. This will allow you to put a plan in place if you anticipate needing assistance finding employment.

	Agency Name	Phone #	Address	Email	Website
1					
2					
3					
4					
5					

It is a good idea to create a *master application*. This is simply a form with all your correct information filled in. You can take this with you and use it when filling out job applications. Having a master application will ensure you are putting the same information on all the applications you fill out. It will also make it easier to fill out applications because you will not have to try and remember past jobs and dates each time; instead, you can simply refer to your master application. It's important to make sure your resume matches the information on your application. Many employers request a copy of your resume be attached to the application.

Remember to list your prison jobs on the application. It can be difficult to get information from the prison after you release, so it's important for you to think of everything you might need prior to your release. Getting copies of your work history and, if possible, your work evaluations will be helpful when completing applications and putting together your job search documents.

MASTER APPLICATION WORKSHEET

Name: _____
Mailing address: _____
Telephone 1: _____
Telephone 2: _____
Email address: _____
Social Security number: _____
Type of job desired: Full-time ____ Part-time ____ Temporary: ____
Position desired: _____
Minimum salary: _____

Education

High school/GED: _____
School location: _____
Years completed: _____
Did you graduate?: _____

****

Trade school name: _____
School location: _____
Years completed: _____
Did you graduate?: _____
Describe any specialized training you may have received:
_____

****

College: _____
School location: _____
Years completed: _____
Did you graduate? _____
Degree obtained: _____

****

Graduate/professional school: _____
School location: _____
Years completed: _____
Did you graduate? _____
Degree obtained: _____

****

Describe any occupational licenses or certifications you have below:
_____

Employment History (list most recent employer first)

Employer name: _____

Employer address: _____

Telephone: _____

Job title: _____

Major responsibilities: _____

Dates employed: From: _____ To: _____

Supervisor's name: _____

May we contact? _____

Reason for leaving: _____

Ending salary: _____

****

Employer name: _____

Employer address: _____

Telephone: _____

Job title: _____

Major responsibilities: _____

Dates employed: From: _____ To: _____

Supervisor's name: _____

May we contact? _____

Reason for leaving: _____

Ending salary: _____

****

Employer name: _____

Employer address: _____

Telephone: _____

Job title: _____

Major responsibilities: _____

Dates employed: From: _____ To: _____

Supervisor's name: _____

May we contact? _____

Reason for leaving: _____

Ending salary: _____

****

Employer name: _____
Employer address: _____
Telephone: _____
Job title: _____
Major responsibilities: _____
Dates employed: From: _____ To: _____
Supervisor's name: _____
May we contact? _____
Reason for leaving: _____
Ending salary: _____

References
Name: _____
Telephone: _____
Name: _____
Telephone: _____
Name: _____
Telephone: _____

Do you have any felony convictions?: ____Please explain:_____

Something that will be good for you to practice before you're sitting in front of an employer is how you will answer questions about your criminal background. Some employers have joined the "Ban the Box" movement and removed the criminal background question from their application. These employers have realized that having this question on the application and deciding whether or not to interview someone based on their answer limits their pool of qualified applicants. Not all employers who have this question on their application will automatically discard an application of someone who has a background, but if they have a qualified applicant with a background and a qualified applicant without, they are more likely to choose the one without. If an application doesn't ask about criminal background, the employer will more than likely ask about your past during the interview.

When you're called in for an interview, you have a few minutes to make your best impression on the employer and land the job. It's a good idea to practice talking about your background to make sure you present the information in the best way possible. When an employer asks you to explain your background, a good way to start is making an "I" statement that tells the employer you've taken responsibility. It can be something as simple as *When I was younger, I made some mistakes.* Drawing attention to how long ago your crime was can be beneficial, for example, *Over five/ten/fifteen years ago, I made some mistakes.* Depending on your crime, you could follow that with something like, *And I took something that didn't belong to me* or *And I got involved in selling illegal substances.* Then you move right in to how you have changed and what all you have done to better yourself since then. Don't spend a lot of time or go into all the details about your crimes. An employer's main concern is who you are today and what kind of employee you will be if they hire you. Not giving all the details but making sure you give enough information so the employer doesn't feel you are minimizing what you did can be a little tricky. That is why it is important for you to practice talking about your background before you are sitting in front of an employer.

Once you have mastered how you will talk about your background at the interview, there are some other common questions you can also prepare yourself for. You might be asked about your goals and where you see yourself in five years. You might be asked to talk about your strengths and weaknesses. Employers will also likely ask why you want to work for their company. It's always a good idea to do a little research on the companies where you're applying. This may seem overwhelming if you're putting in a bunch of applications just trying to get a job. If you don't research them before you apply, make sure you learn a little about them if you get called in for an interview.

Common Interview Questions

1. Why are you here today?
2. Where do you see yourself in five years?
3. Why did you choose this company?
4. Why are you the best person for this position?
5. How do you handle conflict?
6. What would you consider to be a weakness for you?
7. What are your salary expectations?
8. Your application indicates you have a criminal conviction. Can you explain this, please?
9. Are drugs and/or alcohol a problem for you?
10. What were some things you did in prison to occupy your time?
11. Do you have any questions for me?

If the job application asks about a criminal background and asks you to explain, here are some suggestions of what to do:

- Simple: Please allow me to explain in an interview.
- Emphasizes how long ago: I made a mistake over five/ten/fifteen/etc. years ago and would like the opportunity to explain in an interview.
- Drugs: My conviction was related to the manufacturing/utilization/distribution of unhealthy substances. I would like to explain more in an interview.
- Theft: I took something that didn't belong to me. I would like to explain more in an interview.
- Assault: I got into an altercation with another person. I would like to explain more in an interview.

Employers expect honesty. If you are dishonest on your application, you will give the employer the impression that you are a dishonest person, and more than likely you will not be called for an interview. But, remember, you want to be honest on the application without saying too much. Stating all the details of your crime on the application may greatly reduce your chances of an interview. You want the opportunity to speak to the employer in person so they can see you as a person who made a mistake and not just a criminal who doesn't deserve a second chance.

At the interview:

Employer: On your application you indicated you have a criminal conviction. Can you explain this please?

You: (Remember, how you present your situation *does* make a difference.)
Be direct about your conviction, but say what you've done since then, and then finish with how you've changed.

(examples on next page)

Do's

- **Do** be to the point: "I was convicted of burglary in 1997. I took something that didn't belong to me."
- **Do** mention your age or length of time it's been since it happened (if it has been awhile): "When I was 17, I was convicted of car theft."
- **Do** say what you've done since then: "I was convicted of drug possession. I've completed a rehab program, and I don't have that problem anymore. I brought some reference letters for you to look at."
- **Do** show that you're not a threat if your crime involved violence: "I was convicted of assault. I received counseling for managing my anger, and I have a reference letter from my counselor."
- **Do** show that your arrest was not related to your work: "I was convicted of DWI, but I never drank while on the job. I completed a program and have a reference letter from my counselor."
- **Do** take responsibility for your actions: "I made some bad decisions. I regret them very much. I haven't had any problems in the last three years. I have a letter from my probation officer."

Don'ts

- **Don't** give too many details. Instead of saying, "I was going through a lot of stress at the time, with trying to keep custody of my son, and my mother was sick," simply say, "I had family problems and made some poor decisions when trying to cope with them."
- **Don't** explain things by shifting the blame: "I was going to return the things I took, but they didn't give me the chance." Instead, say, "I knew right away that what I did was wrong. I've grown up a lot since then. Here's a letter from my probation officer."
- **Don't** mention a history of addiction unless it's part of the crime and you can show you have maintained sobriety for a length of time. Rather than "I needed the money because I was on drugs at the time," try, "The way I was living then is not the way I'm living now."

If you talk to others who have released from prison, they might say that getting a job is easy but keeping a job is hard. This is an accurate statement. When the job market is good and everyone is hiring, you will be able to get a job. Whether or not you keep your job is completely up to you. There are several factors to consider here. One of the biggest assets to an employer is dependability. They want to hire someone who can and will show up on time for work every day. Of course, after you show up, being productive is important as well. What are the factors that determine whether or not you will show up for work every day? One of the obvious factors is transportation. Do you have a dependable way to get work? Believe it or not, some people get a job and then scramble to find transportation each and every day. Ideally, you will have some type of transportation secured and avoid the stress of scrambling.

Another factor that contributes to how long you stay at a job is whether or not you like the work you're doing. It seems obvious that if you don't like the work, you won't do it for long. Some feel that no job is better than a job you hate doing. This will be another opportunity to do your T.R.U.T.H. work and figure out what will serve you best in reaching your goals. If you find yourself working a job you don't particularly like, one way to think of it is as a stepping-stone to get to the next, better job. Each job you have will build your resume and become a reference for your next job. Keep this in mind as you focus on and advance towards your dream job.

What is your dream job? Are you one of the many who haven't yet figured out what they'd really like to do? There's no need to worry. Most people happen into their career, meaning they get a job that leads to another job or promotion that then leads to another. It's getting that first job that initiates the thoughts, feelings, and actions that leads to the next. It's important not to put limitations on yourself. Don't allow limiting thoughts to block opportunities. Thoughts like, "I'm a felon so no one will hire me," or, "I will never have a high paying job because of my background," are limiting thoughts and can actually keep you from recognizing opportunities.

T.R.U.T.H. work example

T — The Thing is that you've been home for a couple of weeks, and finally an employer has called you in for an interview. It's a fast-food restaurant. R — Recognize your thoughts about this job. *I've put in at least twenty applications and was hoping something other than fast food would call. It doesn't pay enough for me to be able to live on my own. I need a job that pays better* (or) *I have to get a job and sooner is better than later. It's not like my phone is blowing up with employers calling me back.* U — Understand your feelings when you think about taking this job. *I will feel embarrassed to see my friends and serve them a burger. I feel like a failure starting all over* (or) *I will feel more independent if I have my own money. I will feel accomplished if I can pay my family back for some of the help they've given me.* T — Think about your actions. *I'm going to pass on this job and wait for something better* (or) *I will take this job so I can support myself.* H — How will each of these actions serve you? Only you can decide that.

Chapter Notes & Key Takeaways:
-

Chapter 8

Support Systems

Research continues to show that the number-one contributor to being successful after release, even above employment and basic needs, is having a good support system. Who are the people you know you can count on to help you? Who are the people who will support you, encourage you, and offer you advice that's in your best interest? Who are the people you know who love you and want to see you succeed? These are all the type of people you want on your support team. It is important to identify those who will be good teammates for you. It is equally important to identify those who will not.

First, let's think about who you need on your team. Family is an obvious first thought for most. Your parents, your siblings, your extended family, your spouse, and/or your children seem like a great place to start building your support circle. Your support circle comes with certain qualifications that members must meet. It's kind of like you are the employer and you're trying to fill some positions at your business with good, qualified employees. In this case, your business is your life, and the positions that need to be filled are all ones that build into your life. Write down everyone you can think of as possible candidates to fill one of your positions. Now, think about each person on your list and ask these questions:

1. Can I count on this person? Are they dependable?
2. Does this person support and encourage me and want what's best for me?
3. Does this person love me and want to see me succeed?

Answering yes to just one of these questions may qualify that person to be in your support circle. Having a mix of people who are dependable, encouraging, and truly want you to succeed is ideal.

While family may be an obvious choice for some, there are several other good options to consider when creating your support circle. Think outside of your family and into your community. Other candidates for your support circle might be someone you know from church, a past teacher or coach, your AA or NA sponsor, your neighbor, or a counselor or someone involved in your release planning. If you're going to be on probation after you release, you should consider your probation officer as part of your support circle.

Once you have identified who you want in your support circle, have a conversation with them about this. You could do this during a visit or over the phone, but I encourage you to write them a letter. This letter can detail why you chose them to be in your support circle and what they can do to support you after you release. You can also share your goals and desires for your life after release. This will help them get a clear picture of exactly what you are needing from them.

For obvious reasons, you should distance yourself from people who do not have your best interest in mind. This may include old friends or even family members. I have talked to many people who returned to prison after violating their probation and, according to them, the number one reason they violated was because they returned to the same people, places, and activities as before.

HOW TO CHOOSE YOUR SUPPORT TEAM MEMBERS

Consider people who are already in your life or who you will have contact with on a regular basis after you release. Try to think of at least five people. Common relationships that come to mind are role models such as a pastor, a neighbor, a family member, or professionals such as your probation officer or treatment provider.

	Name of person	Relationship to me	Phone number	address	Why I want them on my team	Date I asked them to be on my team
1						
2						
3						
4						
5						

Chapter Notes & Key Takeaways:

Chapter 9

Health

Physical Health

One of the most important ways we take care of ourselves is by taking care of our bodies. The first thing that comes to mind for most of us is a healthy diet and exercise. Most of us also realize that this is way easier said than done. Being in an environment where what you eat and when you can exercise is determined for you adds to the difficulty of accomplishing this. Please don't let that be your excuse to downplay the importance of your physical health. You may have to get creative to figure out what kind of plan you can put in place that is best for your health. What healthy food options do you have? What kind of schedule can you create to get some exercise?

While some people like to work on their fitness goals alone, others find it helpful to have another person to do this with. This may be beneficial if you would like to lose weight. Having someone besides ourselves to hold us accountable will oftentimes keep us on track. This is also helpful when exercising. When you have a workout partner, you can provide motivation and encouragement to each other. Whether you do it alone or you buddy up with someone, the important thing is to make those simple, everyday decisions that contribute to your physical well-being.

If you have access to a recreation department at your facility, find out if they offer structured exercise programs or any other physical fitness activities. If they do, I encourage you to join one. Recreation staff may also have recommendations on exercises and nutrition that fit your current situation. Once again, it doesn't hurt to ask.

Often times, just writing down what you're eating every day will help you identify unhealthy eating habits. If you desire to lose weight, this is a great practice.

My Daily Food Log

Day of week	Breakfast	Snack	Lunch	Snack	Dinner	Snack
Sunday						
Monday						
Tuesday						
Wednesday						
Thursday						
Friday						
Saturday						

If you are an exercise beginner, there is nothing wrong with easing into your physical activity routine. A simple walk is better than lying in bed all day. It doesn't matter how you get started as long as you get started.

Exercise/physical activity log

Day of week	Type of exercise	Length of time or number of reps
Sunday		
Monday		
Tuesday		
Wednesday		
Thursday		
Friday		
Saturday		

Mental Health

When we think of someone being healthy, it's typically physical health that comes to mind. We all have an idea of what a healthy person looks like. The part of a person's health that we can't always see is their mental state or mental health. Just because our mental health is not as visible as our physical health does not make it any less important. In fact, many will agree that good mental health is a prerequisite for good physical health.

Good mental health requires us to focus on ourselves and what we need in order to feel our best. Part 1 of this book gives examples of different ways to focus on ourselves. It is important to know when you need to take a mental break. Most of the time our body will signal us when we need to do this. For instance, if you find yourself reacting to something differently than you typically would, maybe you need to step away and process your thoughts. Another example could be needing some time alone after you've spent the whole day in a large group of people. Or the truth may be the opposite of that; after you've spent a lot of time alone, you may need to interact with someone.

Stress is a common feeling that every human being experiences from time to time. Our body is very good at letting us know when we are feeling stressed. Some signs of stress we may experience are a racing heart, sweating, pacing, running our hands through our hair, biting our nails, fidgeting, or hyperventilating, just to name a few. Stress affects our mental health. Since everyone experiences stress, having stress-relief tools is important and will definitely decrease the effects of stress on our body.

Stress-Relief Tips
(For short-term or long-term stress relief)

1. Take one to two deep breaths. This alone will help you relax and let go of stress.
2. Imagine a person, place, or thing that makes you happy and focus on it.
3. Meditate.
4. Create something.
5. Work on a hobby or something else you love doing.
6. Talk to someone you love.
7. Exercise.
8. Eat a balanced diet.
9. Take a walk.
10. Get out in nature.
11. Listen to music.
12. Read a book.
13. Practice positive self-talk.
14. Find things to be grateful for.
15. Get a massage.

Healthcare After Release

Having access to healthcare, both physical and mental, is something every person needs. Unfortunately, this can be expensive, which prevents some from receiving the care they need. There are resources available that will assist with the cost and/or provide insurance coverage. It is very important for you to research these options to make sure you know how to access healthcare resources should you need them.

There are four basic options to help meet your healthcare needs. These are employer-provided insurance, Medicaid, Medicare, Affordable Care Act coverage, or sliding-scale clinics. Here's a brief overview of each.

Many companies have a health insurance plan for their employees. This varies from employer to employer. Some offer this coverage free of charge to their employees. Most, however, pay a percentage of the premium and the employee pays the rest. Large corporations may have several plan options to choose from. And with most, you can choose to insure just yourself or add your spouse and children. Some companies may offer immediate access to this coverage when you start working for them. Others may have a set number of days you have to work for them before you are eligible to enroll in their insurance plan. Insurance coverage is one of the benefits you should research when doing your job search.

Medicaid is a state healthcare coverage program. This money is distributed by the federal government to each state. States receive individual amounts based on several factors to include population and poverty statistics. Each state has its own application process. Medicaid provides very low cost, or even free, medical coverage to qualifying individuals. Felons can qualify for Medicaid. You can apply through your local social services office, sometimes called family services.

The Affordable Care Act (ACA) is the healthcare reform signed into law by President Barack Obama in 2010. Also known as Obamacare, the intention was to extend health-insurance coverage to millions of uninsured Americans. Healthcare.gov is website that details everything about the ACA and how to enroll. There are four categories of health insurance plans: bronze, silver, gold, and platinum. Each plan offers different coverage at a different out-of-pocket cost to you. Basically, you pay a monthly bill to your insurance company (called a "premium"), even if you don't use medical services that month. You pay out-of-pocket costs, including a deductible, when you get care. It's important to think about both kinds of costs when shopping for a plan.

Lastly, most communities have a medical provider that offers services on a sliding scale based on your income. You need to find out if there is a facility like this in your community. These facilities may offer medical, mental health, and/or dental services. While health insurance may be the most long-term, comprehensive option, these sliding-scale facilities are a great option if you do not have any coverage.

Chapter Notes & Key Takeaways:
-

Chapter 10

Communication Styles and Problem Solving

Communication is much more than two people exchanging words. How we communicate with each other is a primary factor in what determines how good (or bad) our relationships are. This includes relationships with our significant other, our children, our friends, our boss, etc. Communication affects every single relationship we have. This is why it's so important to understand how you are communicating.

When you think about your communication style, don't just think about how words come out of your mouth. Communication is more than that. It includes what you say, how you say it, how you listen, how you comprehend, and your body language. Everyone communicates differently. While there are some definite good communication skills and bad communication habits, there is a lot of room in the middle to develop your unique communication technique.

Most of us have been told about or have read about the four basic communication styles. These are passive, assertive, passive-aggressive, and aggressive. All communication falls into one of these styles. I'm going to give a brief description of each style. If you want to learn more about how to be an effective communicator, there are many great books that go into greater detail about each communication style and how to communicate with people from each of them.

When you think of passive communicators, think of the people in your life who suppress their thoughts and feelings and never express them. This often results in a build-up of anger or resentment that seems out of character for them. Passive communicators tend to give in to other people and seem to just go with the flow. It seems as though they are incapable of saying no.

Now, think of the people in your life who typically dominate conversations. They are known as aggressive communicators. They tend to focus the conversation on themselves. They interrupt others and are poor listeners. They may even use intimidation techniques to get their point across.

The next communication style is passive-aggressive. Just like its name, it is a combination of those two communication styles. If you use this communication style you appear passive and find subtle ways to let your resentment come out. A lot of sarcasm is a sign of this type of communication style. It's when body language doesn't match the words you're speaking, such as saying, "I didn't mind that at all," but with an angry look on your face.

Assertive commutators have figured out the most effective way to express themselves. They can confidently express their needs and desires. They listen while others speak. Unlike passive communicators, they have the ability to say no. They have mastered using "I" statements, such as "I feel sad and lonely when I can't talk to you." This communication style respects the opinions of others.

Problem solving is a skill that we must develop. I'm sure you've noticed the difference between people who are good problem solvers and those who aren't. Some have mastered this skill and there is no problem they can't solve. Most of us are still developing this skill and are good at solving some problems while others are still challenging. Ironically, we must experience problems to become good at solving them. The next time you have a problem that is challenging you, don't get upset and feel helpless. Instead, recognize this as an opportunity to work on and improve your problem-solving skills.

How do we know when we're having a problem? Our body gives us warning signs, which may include a racing heart, red face, sweating, etc. Once we realize we're having a problem, we move on to our thoughts about the problem and how they are making us feel. Does this sound familiar? Hopefully you recognize this process as the T.R.U.T.H. tool. You can use the T.R.U.T.H. tool to work through any problem. Some problems may require immediate action, while others give us time to think. The goal is to become so familiar with the T.R.U.T.H. tool that you use it automatically when faced with any type of problem.

Using the T.R.U.T.H. Tool to help problem solve:

T — The Thing, or in this case the problem:

R — Realize thoughts you're having about the problem:

U — Understand that your feelings are based on your thoughts:

T — Take Action based on your thoughts and feelings:

H — How will/did that serve you:

Chapter Notes & Key Takeaways:

Conclusion

During my correctional career, I encountered many inmates who needed assistance in addressing barriers that they knew would hinder their release in some way. Some of these barriers prevented inmates from leaving prison as early as they otherwise could have. Some of these barriers were waiting to be addressed as soon as they got home from prison. The bottom line is, if you had an issue with something prior to coming to prison, it will most likely be waiting for you when you release unless you resolve it before then.

The whole purpose of this book is to give you the power and control to resolve these barriers yourself. It's not always easy to get the assistance necessary from staff, and your family has to manage their own lives, which are typically busy enough. If you don't have a way to get on the internet, then you will probably have to ask someone to look up an agency's contact information for you. If you have to ask someone to look up an address for you, for example your local Job Center, explain that you need the address so you can write them and ask about programs and resources that might help you when you release.

This book is intended to help you realize that you are the only person in control of your life. Maybe your current situation feels completely out of your control, but I encourage you to look deeper into what control really means. You may not have control over when you eat or where you go right now, but I assure you, you do still have control over your life. You have complete control over your thoughts, feelings, and actions, no matter the situation. Knowing this and living from this place is where true control comes from.

If you practice the tools in Part 1 of this book and use the tools in Part 2, it will become apparent that you have been in control of your life the whole time. Where you are today is a result of your decisions. This is true for all of us. You and only you can make your best (or worst) life happen. Now that you know this, I hope you will do the necessary work to address any barriers that will hinder you after you release. Please always remember, your best life awaits, so do your T.R.U.T.H. work and make it happen. I sincerely wish you the very best.

Bibliography

John C. Maxwell, *15 Invaluable Laws of Growth*
Brene Brown, Listening to shame | Brené Brown - YouTube
Brooke Castillo, The Life Coach School Podcast
Jeff Olson, *The Slight Edge*
The Missouri Job Center, employment resources

Acknowledgements

I am grateful for the thousands of inmates I worked with over the course of my career. They helped me become who I am today.

I am grateful for my four children and their beautiful souls. They keep me motivated and help me practice my problem-solving skills.

I am grateful for my dear friend, Lisa. She convinced me this workbook was relevant and necessary — and then convinced me to write it.

I am grateful for my wonderful wife, Amy. Her unfailing support and encouragement help keep me on a path to my best life.

About the Author

After a 20-year career with the Federal Bureau of Prisons, Lisa Landrigan retired and created her own business, Cornerstone Consulting Services. This business provides life coaching to individuals and products and services to prisons and jails, universities and criminal justice professionals. Her business created a one-of-a-kind software called *Consider This Life*. This computer "game" helps incarcerated persons prepare for release by allowing them to play out their life decisions as practice before the real decisions have to be made.

www.ingramcontent.com/pod-product-compliance
Lightning Source LLC
Chambersburg PA
CBHW081156290426
44108CB00018B/2570